Spilled Milk

Wisdom And Wisecracks For The Brokenhearted

Kit Campbell

iUniverse, Inc.
New York   Bloomington

Spilled Milk
Wisdom And Wisecracks For The Brokenhearted

Copyright © 2009 by Kit Campbell.

All rights reserved. No part of this book may be used or reproduced by any means, graphic, electronic, or mechanical, including photocopying, recording, taping or by any information storage retrieval system without the written permission of the publisher except in the case of brief quotations embodied in critical articles and reviews.

The views expressed in this work are solely those of the author and do not necessarily reflect the views of the publisher, and the publisher hereby disclaims any responsibility for them.

iUniverse books may be ordered through booksellers or by contacting:

iUniverse
1663 Liberty Drive
Bloomington, IN 47403
www.iuniverse.com
1-800-Authors (1-800-288-4677)

Because of the dynamic nature of the Internet, any Web addresses or links contained in this book may have changed since publication and may no longer be valid.

ISBN: 978-1-4401-4299-4 (pbk)
ISBN: 978-1-4401-4300-7 (ebk)

Printed in the United States of America

iUniverse rev. date: 6/24/2009

For Mom,
For Everything
I Love You

Contents

COMMON GROUND 1

HIS LOSS 3

WHISKEY AND CIGARETTES 6

MIND OVER MATTER. 9

THIS TOO 13

LEMONS INTO LEMONADE 16

HAIR OF THE DOG 19

RAISING THE BAR 22

ON HOLIDAY 25

LIVING LIFE 28

TICK TOCK 30

LOVE OR MONEY 35

ERROR 38

WHAT ABOUT YOUR FRIENDS?. 44

HERE WE GO AGAIN. 47

TOO GOOD. 50

MAD NOT SAD 54

YOU SO CRAZY. 57

BURY THE HATCHET 61

LITTLE MISS REBOUND 64

REPEAT OFFENDERS 67

WHAT IT IS 72

GO TEAM GO 75

THE KEYMASTER. 78

IN THE DARK 81

MAKE THAT MOVE 84

PRESERVATIVES ADDED 87

KEEPING THE FAITH 89

ACKNOWLEDGEMENTS 91

Common Ground

I wish I could find a better word than 'snowflakes' to describe the relationships we have with men on every level. In fact, I'm sure there has got to be a better word but I just can't seem to put my finger on it. But there is no way that they could ever be the same; the relationships, that is. Sure, they may be alike, but never just the same. Varying factors like those involved and action versus reaction keep them from being one in the same.

Think back as far as your mind takes you and remember where it started. Everyone had a kindergarten boyfriend whose name their mother's would taunt them with, didn't they? Mine was John Travolta as Danny Zuko in Grease.

By second grade, my real life classmates, Joey, Henry and James taught me a valuable lesson. Henry was the first to call me his girlfriend during recess but obviously wasn't around much because somehow James was able to woo me with jewelry he had stolen from his mother. The next thing I knew, Joey kissed me on the lips and the naked pictures we drew later that day, landed us in the principal's office with our parents. The lesson: boys are nothing but trouble.

But they are fun, aren't they? I think it's safe to say there was a tomboy period in my grammar school years. Why stand by the bike rack and converse when your brothers and their friends were playing Bounce N' Fly? That right there was a lesson in restraint: who you were allowed to have feelings for and who you were not. Certainly my brothers' friends were off limits, but admiring them without anyone knowing was fine, at that point.

Jr. High was when most of the girls were spraying their bangs up high and loading on unsightly globs of mascara to catch the boys' eyes. I, however, spent most of my time getting Slurpees with my girlfriends. Aside from weekly episodes of 90210, we didn't find much use for boys.

Kit Campbell

We were too busy finding out what was going on with us before we cared about what was going on with them.

High school and the years that followed are kind of a blur and certainly not my finest hour. Sex was not valuable or even meaningful, which saddens me now. Adolescent emotions drown by underage drinking bore constant conflict. It was a whirlwind of Me versus you, Me versus Me and then Me versus everyone. Zero productive and/or healthy relationships were established during those years. While it's not my favorite time to look back on, I take full responsibility for my poor choices. What a waste, really.

But my twenties have certainly been a different story completely. They've been somewhat healthy and happy, which is all you could hope for. Not only becoming comfortable of being in your own skin, honestly enjoying every ounce of what you are. Is that how it happened for you? Is that when you changed your mind and believed that every year just keeps getting better? That's how it's been for me.

No matter how old you are when that transition is complete, that's when the next thing that happens is really big. Whether or not you've spent time in shoes like mine, I'll bet we do have one thing in common. In fact, it's probably the one thing that pretty much everyone has in common. The one thing: "the one".

I'll bet that you remember everything about that person. You remember how crazy about them you were and how astonished you were when everything had fallen in place so nicely. It's crystal clear in my memory.

Do you recall how happy and hopeful he made you feel? And how amazingly you voluntarily could not see your life without them? How you were so sure you'd be with this person forever?

Now let me ask you one more thing. Do you remember what it felt like when you found out that you were wrong?

HIS LOSS

Don't you just hate it when people try to comfort you after a breakup by saying that it's his loss? It's gotten to a point where it's so clichéd that no one wants to hear it anymore. But if you break it down, there is wisdom in those words. It's something that I completely analyzed over and over again, before allowing it to help me get by.

Losing Perry was something I'd have to describe as the biggest loss in my life so far. This was someone I thought I was going to marry. Not even as a pipe dream, he was the one who put the thought in my head. We'd been checking out houses together. I knew this was the man who was going to give me my kids. And then, after painting a beautiful picture of things to come, he changed his mind. Suddenly, he didn't know for sure if I was the one he was supposed to be with forever. He wanted to leave. And how do you argue with that?

Believe me, I tried. I begged Perry to reconsider. I warned him that he'd never find anyone better. "I'm supposed to be with you," I would tell him. "Don't you think I know that?" No amount of tears or words would bring him to his senses. And that was the end of us.

I was a wreck. I didn't leave my bed for three days and I couldn't eat. My eyes were almost swollen shut from crying and it honestly felt like I was going to die. Yeah, I guess you could say I suffered a pretty major loss.

While he did call and check on me from time to time, he didn't even seem upset with the situation. He actually told me that he tried his best not to think about it. I certainly didn't have that luxury. It was the first and only thought in my mind during my waking hours and dreams of him tormented me in my sleep.

For weeks after we broke up, Perry was still telling me that he loved me and that he wasn't sure exactly what he was doing. He thought time away would make him miss me, but no such luck. He told me that the

3

last time he dropped me off at home, he felt like he was leaving a funeral. I told him he was right, because something really good just died.

I know what you're thinking. How do you figure his loss was greater than mine? What was I losing? A man that stopped loving me? That doesn't sound so bad, right? No big deal.

That's not to take anything away from him. He was a great boyfriend and truly the love of my life. He used to drive an hour to surprise me at work just to give me a kiss goodnight and he'd buy flowers for no reason at all. My family loved him and I was proud to show him off wherever we'd go. He took me so many places I'd never been before and we always had so much fun. He'd call to say good morning and again to say goodnight. He was always making me laugh and for a while there, he really did love me.

Although he will remain the biggest loss of my life, I believe that his loss was worse in the long run.

Let's face it, I lost someone who fell out of love with me and he lost someone who will always love him. Sounds like a bad move on his part, doesn't it? Sure, he doesn't have to check in with anyone anymore. No one is nagging him about not spending enough time together. He doesn't have to remember anyone's birthday or anniversary. And he can always chose poker night over other plans from now on. He has his freedom back completely.

But I'll tell you what he doesn't have. He doesn't have someone to depend on like he used to. He doesn't have someone to listen to him vent when he's stressed out or upset. He doesn't have someone to drive fifty miles out of her way to spend the night with him. There will be no more back rubs after a long day's work and no more breakfast in bed. He doesn't get to wake up next to that sweet smell anymore. He no longer has someone to confide in. When his friends blow him off last minute on his birthday, I won't be there. He doesn't have someone to make him lunches that make his entire crew jealous and he doesn't have someone to take him to the butt doctor when he needs to go.

The butt doctor? Yeah, that's right. I said it. He's losing the only person in his life that he could count on to take him to such a place. He

Spilled Milk

knew I was the only one who would joke with him about it privately, yet he could trust to tell what was really going on. He knew he could rely on me to be there when the doctor needs someone to report back to. Is it horrible that I'm drawing attention to his embarrassing little procedure? Possibly, but it's only to prove a point. Funny as it may seem, if I for some ungodly reason required a visit to my friendly, neighborhood butt doctor, I have plenty of people to call on for help.

I have incredibly caring and reliable friends and family. But he doesn't. When he told his mother about his procedure, the only thing she wanted to know was who was taking him. Can you guess who he said? Bingo. He was losing the only person in his life who was genuinely concerned about him. I certainly hope he didn't have any follow up appointments. What a catastrophe that must have been!

I would have done anything for him and he knew that. And now, if you catch me on a good day, I'd take it into consideration, at best. So the fact of the matter is, that he lost a girl that would have walked through fire to get to him, he lost the love of his life. Yes, I too lost the love of my life, but only because he chose to give me up. I love him more than anyone ever did and I'm convinced I loved him more than anyone ever will. So when you do the math, he's the one that comes up short. His is truly the greater loss.

WHISKEY AND CIGARETTES

My first brush with true heartache was agony, as it is for everyone. I was in college, working full time and had just secured an internship at an incredibly popular radio station. Needless to say, I didn't have time to grieve. I traveled between three cities that were at least an hour apart every single day, so finding alone time to sit around and cry just wasn't an option. I had things to do.

Instead, I locked it all away and continued on with my busy life. After all, there was work to be done and connections to be made. I found myself surrounded by an entirely new crowd of people. Before I knew it, I was the popular girl on the scene, trading my opportunity to sleep for nights filled with whiskey and cigarettes. The attention I was getting from my new group of admirers, along with the intoxication that followed, was certainly helping my heartache fade, so like any brokenhearted girl, I pressed on.

My list of conquests was growing by the day, but I paid that no attention. I hid behind dark glasses for the rest of the year and tried to maintain some form of balance. My occurrences with the opposite sex lasted no longer than a night or two and my meals became predominantly liquid. It wasn't until I consciously realized that I kept a plastic bag in the console of my car in case I had to get sick while I was on the road, that I discovered that slowing down my lifestyle might have been a good idea.

I took a painful break from the blur. Drying out was no picnic. I cried myself to sleep a few times and moved forward. Somewhere in the clearing, I remembered thinking that I wouldn't behave this way again. I couldn't allow myself to get out of control just because I was in pain. After deciding that I could still keep the same crowd, all in moderation of course, I put my nose to the grindstone.

After Perry and I broke up, it made me sick to think of being with another man. Maybe it was because the thought of me with someone

Spilled Milk

else, entitled him to the same experience. Who knows? But for a while, it was a notion I couldn't even stomach.

Valentine's Day came rolling around and like a silly broad, I didn't think I could handle it. It was just another day, right? Just another day I would think of him nonstop.

I went to work and my longtime friend, Josh suggested a night on the town afterward. This wasn't of much interest to me; I just wanted the day to end. Last minute, I called him back and decided to go. Josh's roommate, who was someone I had randomly hooked up with during my drunken escapades two years prior, was coming to pick me up and we were on our way. We made stops along Division Street and after four hours and a lot of liquor, we were headed to the hot tub at their house for a little after hour's adventure.

By that time, we switched to drinking water and began to soak. After nodding off a few times, Josh got out, dried off and was off to bed. That left the roommate and I alone for the first time in a long time. What were we to do?

Suddenly the idea of being with someone else wasn't so bad. More importantly, the desire was there. I had no plans of making the first move but I'll admit I really wanted something to happen. And it did.

Josh couldn't have been in dry clothes yet before the two of us remaining in the tub had started to kiss. Details aside, it was hot as hell. We shared the excitement of something new, the comfort of a friend and the heat that could have started that place on fire. Later we fell asleep in his room and as it turned out, my Valentine's Day wasn't as treacherous as I had feared. I could do this. I was back.

But then it was morning and a surprise 8am visit from the roommate's mother was the last thing either one of us had expected. Poor Josh was sprawled out on the couch in his underwear when she came in. I didn't even leave his bedroom and why? Because it was awkward and those are the moments you fear in a situation like this. You want everything to go smooth and at the end, you've just got a great story to tell; a story that doesn't involve his mother whatsoever.

7

Kit Campbell

It would be different if I had met her before, but that wasn't the case. Besides, I'm sure he didn't want to explain why there's some strange girl coming out of his bedroom with his boxers on. How uncomfortable. I stayed in bed for as long as I could take it but I couldn't fall back asleep.

I got dressed, took a deep breath and headed downstairs. How funny that he introduced me (barely) as Josh's friend! Even funnier is that all I said was, "I gotta go" and left. These two people were just sleeping together and now they are behaving like friendly neighbors. Ah, the art of the one night stand. Wow. I *was* back.

So here I am, once again, taking that 8am walk of shame back to my car with my panties in my pocket. Hot tub excitement with a good looking guy made me feel like a rock star. I was desired again and felt sexy as hell. This is behavior that is easily habit forming. But was this really what I wanted? Hardly. Sure, it was fun while it lasted and it's completely tempting to do over and over again. Not to mention that the memory of what we did will play host to future fantasies, but was that really enough? Would he call me later to see how I was feeling? Or to tell me that he had a great time? No way. So as much as it may have been an immediate comfort and relief, it was temporary and not exactly what I was looking for. Let's aim a little higher, shall we?

MIND OVER MATTER

When you put your emotions aside and look at nothing but the facts, you can begin to make much wiser decisions. That's your moment of clarity. It's the most important step in getting your life back on track.

Enough of this "follow your heart" nonsense! Sometimes matters of the heart cause false hope and illogical thinking, which doesn't always lead to the best for you. So put your brain to work and let your head lead the way. I mean, come on; someone's got to drive this thing.

We need to get our minds out of the clouds just for a minute. Too often we expect destiny to kick in, when instead we should realize that we are all guilty of blaming insignificant coincidences on fate.

This bad habit tormented me for months and I've honestly had to snap myself back into reality a few times since, because it still seems to happen from time to time. Humor me and check out some examples. You'll find that you or someone close to you is guilty of the same damn thing.

Towards the end of the winter the year we broke up, I booked a trip to Cancun with my mom and sister. This was the vacation everyone said I deserved, including Perry. Everyone believed that getting away would help me feel better about everything and possibly clear my mind for a few days. The night before I left, I drove over to Josh's new condo in the loop. Oddly enough, there was a parking spot right out in front, so I pulled in. And whose car do you think I parked behind? Of all the cars in downtown Chicago that night, I just had to park directly and unknowingly behind the man who just broke my heart. My pulse started to race. Could he see me? Did I know I was there? Would he be upset and think I was following him around? Was I making a big deal out of nothing? Should I just laugh it off and leave him a funny note on his windshield? Or will he think that's weird? Do I turn off my ignition and cry? The way I saw it, this was all about choices.

Kit Campbell

It's not a sign, it's a coincidence. That's what I had to tell myself over and over again. In fact, I scribbled it down on notebook paper and set it on my nightstand. It was the last thing I saw before I went to bed and the first thing I saw when I woke up. It helped remind me that I was the only one hurting from this and it would be best to just let it go. It's not a sign, it's a coincidence.

Sure, it was strange that of all the cars in the city that night, he parked in front of my friend's new place and that I ended up right behind him. But was it really fate trying to catch our attention? I doubt it. It was an opportunity to walk past his car and treat it like any other car on the street. But that would just make too much sense, wouldn't it? Instead, I scurried off to Josh's place and obsessed about it for hours. Two days later, I was on a beach in Mexico crying about it. Six long island ice teas later, I finally came to my senses and started to enjoy myself; temporarily. It seemed like a never ending battle.

Take the song "Purple Rain" for instance. I'm not the kind of girl that names a song that represents every guy in her life, but admittedly, this one was ours. I don't even remember how it came to be. Maybe it became our song because when I'd sneak him into work with me, I'd always end up airing it, since it was the longest song on our play list and we wanted to fool around in the studio. Maybe it was because he surprised me with tickets to see Prince live in Champaign the night before Easter. When the purple one gave us his final encore and played our song, Perry wrapped his arms around me and thousands of people just disappeared. It was like the song was being played exclusively for the two of us.

For months after we broke up, I avoided all Prince songs, in fear of breaking down. Then I had a reality check. The radio played Prince long before Perry and they will continue to play his music long after all of this is over. It's as simple as that.

Does it mean that I can't hold a fond memory of these little things? Not at all. I can think of Perry when I hear a song that reminds me of him. After spending so much of my life with him, I've earned that right. But does hearing "Purple Rain" on the radio mean that he's coming

Spilled Milk

back? No way. Does it mean that by some cosmic force he's listening to it at the same time and thinking of me? My guess is probably not. But for some reason, our minds play tricks on us and we end up feeding on false hope. I believe that's truly unhealthy behavior.

When you break up with someone, you find yourself constantly reminded of them; it's only logical. When you spend hours on end, day after day together, you will accumulate experiences and memories. Period. So it makes perfect sense to think of them when random events occur. If you let the memory skip from one end of your mind to the other, it's acceptable, in my opinion. A moment with your head in the clouds is okay, as long as you remember to keep your feet on the ground.

And then there are the times when we indulge ourselves in heartache. When no one's around, you put your song on repeat and look at old pictures of when you were happy together. You feel your eyes welling up with tears when you read the cards he gave you and finally give in and have a good, hard cry. At this point, the pain becomes self-inflicted. He's not causing this pain, you are. Not only are you allowing it, but encouraging it. Snap out of it and get a hold of yourself.

Enter Chicago White Sox. I had been to a few games prior to dating Perry, but didn't become a huge fan until he provoked it. We went to the stadium together every chance we had. It was a given that I'd have to live with his ghost standing next to me at certain events. Whether it was remembering something he always used to say or discovering I was doing the same old things, with someone new by my side. Hell, Chicago went to the World Series and won by a landslide and I was going to celebrate, with or without him. And now, I continue to be a fan, whether it's with friends, my brother or a date. Thoughts of him pass through my mind, but a stolen base or a homerun snaps me right back to where I need to be. He's not here, but I'm still having a blast. How nice.

Come on, girls, let's use our heads. However difficult it may feel, it's really very simple. It happened before and it will happen again. Sure, you parked next to him. He still lives and works in Chicago, right? So deal with it. Park your car and be thankful you didn't have to pop for valet.

Besides, I'm sick of turning off the radio when Aerosmith comes on just because they happen to be his favorite band. Big wow; does that

11

Kit Campbell

mean that I should deprive myself of "Walk This Way"? I don't think so. And I don't think that anyone else should be affected in this way, either. It happened before and it will happen again; just remember that. So go ahead, turn up the radio and sing as loud as you want.

If that's not inspirational enough, remember that nobody wants to be the girl who's still talking about her ex. And even more importantly, nobody wants to be the one who's forced to listen to her. Following your heart isn't always the best advice. It sounds nice and is very sweet, but can sometimes lead you down a rocky road. We should instead use our heads. It's just that simple. When a memory runs across your mind, remember how wonderful things were and leave it there. You can't allow yourself to become an emotional basketcase. You have to maintain control, especially when you feel like giving up. If you need to, go ahead a have a good cry. Then scarf down a candy bar and move on. There's no magical power that is going to put you back where you once were. So deal with it.

We have been blessed with the power to utilize our incredible minds. So use your brain, that's what it's there for. And remember to keep your head up and eyes peeled for the next lucky guy.

THIS TOO

When the going gets tough, you can always count on someone offering their comfort with the ever popular saying, "This Too Shall Pass". Little do most know that phrase comes from an ancient Jewish folktale about King Solomon.

The King once searched for a cure against depression and gathered his wise men. They assembled for meditation and advised him to have a ring made. The ring was to be engraved with the Hebrew words, Gam Ze Yaavor. Solomon followed the advice and wore the ring constantly. Whenever he felt sad or depressed, he looked at the ring, and consequently his mood would change instantly and he would feel cheerful. The saying reminded him to appreciate every passing moment and to continue living his precious life.

This tale has been passed down for thousands of years and its moral has brought comfort to millions. The Hebrew words, Gam Ze Yaavor translate into the philosophical English words we have all come to know; "This Too Shall Pass".

I have always found these words to be comforting, but didn't see how true they really were until just recently. Not long ago, my cousin and I got together after work for a frosty, adult beverage; actually about six of them. The conversation started off like any other, but after a few drinks, we found ourselves discussing the entertaining subject of past partners.

As we sifted through our growing list of lovers, we laughed and reminisced about each and every one of them. We giggled about the situations we used to, and still do, find ourselves in. It was a given that we were going to remember their first names and the order that they fell in chronologically, but then came an amusing question. Do we remember their last names? Did we know them all in the first place?

Kit Campbell

She had me beat, hands down. It was as simple as remembering everyone's full name and she did it. I, on the other hand, didn't have such a great memory. Sure, there was that one guy Brian but I never knew his last name. I didn't ask, he didn't tell and it didn't matter. So it's not like I forgot.

But this is the kicker, someone I held close to my heart at one point, was suddenly a stranger without a name. There was a man I dated for about six months during college, who was responsible for hurting me pretty badly. This was someone I was once very attached to and now found it mildly amusing that I couldn't even remember his name.

The story of he and I isn't scandalous, it's more humiliating because after six months of being together, he disappeared into thin air. No phone calls or explanations came my way, only silence. I was really upset and confused for a long time after he left. It was nowhere near the heartache I have experienced since, but it still hurt nonetheless.

After another round of drinks, we still couldn't figure out his last name. We asked the bartender if he remembered, but it had been some time since we'd been in that watering hole. It was really starting to bother me that I had forgotten his name, so I had no choice but to start making some drunken phone calls. I started with Josh because they'd gone to high school together. Unfortunately, I ended up getting his voicemail, so I left him a message in hopes of hearing back soon with the answer. No such luck.

Before too long, it was last call and still we came up with nothing. After I was home and in bed, I got to thinking. How could I possibly forget this guy? He used to be so important to me and now I can't even remember his name! It's not like thirty years had gone by; it was more like three. I was almost ashamed of myself. Eventually, I drifted into sleep for the night.

It wasn't surprising that I didn't hear my cell phone ring when Josh called me back with the correct answer. After hearing the voicemail he left for me, it was like my memory had finally come back. How embarrassing to not remember him after everything we experienced together. Yes, shame on me.

Spilled Milk

But there was a lesson to be learned. At the time of this guy's disappearance, I was so upset and couldn't wait for the pain to fade away. And now, funny as it may seem, I couldn't even remember his damn name! This was a prime example, though completely unpoetic, of the saying, "This Too Shall Pass".

Putting things into perspective like that reminded me that this heartache from Perry wasn't going to last forever. Next year, I wouldn't even think twice of his birthday coming and going, because I may not even remember what day it falls on. What a comforting thought! Although there are certain things I will never forget, they won't forever be front and center in my mind.

So the next time someone offers you that particular advice, the last thing you should do is ignore it. Do yourself a favor and really listen to those words. Consider what they mean to you. This pain isn't going to last. And it's alright to actually continue finding value in the moments of your life. Say it to yourself. This too shall pass. This too shall pass. Before you know it, you will no longer be concerned with what's-his-name.

LEMONS INTO LEMONADE

Working as a producer for a popular radio call in show that revolves around love and relationships, I've spoken to people from all walks of life on the subject. I've heard it all. From your usual "we've grown apart" to the scandalous "I caught him cheating" to the unbelievable "she was a man". As strange as it may seem, our callers aren't hungry for attention and don't call to be in the spotlight. They call in because they honestly believe that we can help them.

We've always maintained that we are not psychologists, we're disc jockeys. We offer our opinion, perhaps some advice and we play them a song. While some of the stories are touching and can really hit home, I've always kept a pretty good sense of humor about all of it. Because as we all know, if there's one thing out there that is capable of messing you up completely, it's love.

I've spoken to them all: the abused housewife that keeps taking him back and the widower that wants company but allows guilt to stand in the way of meeting anyone new. And while my heart would love to offer them each a helping hand, my head always helped me to roll my eyes and laugh it off.

Perry used to come to work with me quite a bit. On the weekends, we could spend time in private and due to our hectic schedules, it really helped. I'd bring dinner and we'd have studio picnics. We'd cuddle up a little, sing along to some of the music and sometimes even take some calls just for fun. We'd joke about how crazy the listeners sounded, not knowing that everything we had would fall apart, just as it did for the callers.

Just as our relationship began to crumble, my career changed lanes without signaling. The station I was working for had flipped formats and suddenly played nothing but classic R&B love songs.

Spilled Milk

The entire on-air staff was terminated, leaving the host of the evening program and myself in uncharted waters. Everyone around me was leaving, including my love and it really felt like my world was falling apart. After hours of being alone in the studio, I wondered if I had somehow enraged our higher power. Listening to love songs for days on end after I was abandoned without reason, seemed like some kind of sick, ironic punishment.

The life I was barely living at the time started to take a toll on my work and vice versa. Suddenly every choice I made wasn't so shallow and apathetic. I poured my emotions into the show, whether it was scriptwriting for the host or straight programming. It was a healthy release in a forum designed for such feelings. This was not going to be my demise, this was going to work for me. Best of all, the city was going for it.

Our ratings shot up in the first trend and I was rewarded shortly thereafter. While my superiors congratulated me for my creativity, I realized there was a light at the end of the tunnel. Everything I had been through in my personal life was actually making me better in my professional life. That was the first ray of light after a rather long blackout.

I was suddenly so much more sensitive to what our callers were going through. So many of them utilized me as a coach to get past the hard times they were facing. And nothing pleased me more than the opportunity to make a change in someone's life that desperately needed it.

To be honest, the women in Chicago weren't working very hard to get what they deserved. Although it's with a great deal of joy that I offer bits of encouragement and self respect to those who just need a push in the right direction. No matter if it was as simple as reminding a young girl that she doesn't need to take back a cheating boyfriend or if it was as serious as recommending a shelter to a battered wife, I felt like I was starting to make a tiny little difference in Chicago. It was nothing earth shattering, but it felt healthy. It felt good.

This really put my "end of the world" theory to rest. See, I have this theory that used to bother me quite a bit. If the end of the world

Kit Campbell

happens tomorrow and we're left to fend for ourselves, do you consider yourself a survivor? How long would you last? While my father and brothers carry the talents of a carpenter, plumber, electrician and award winning hunter, it looks like we're off to a great start. My mom is a nurse, so no further explanation is needed there. And then there's me. While my family flourishes in rebuilding their lives, hypothetically, what am I supposed to do? Put on an album so that can tap their feet as they work? How unimportant my job seems when you look at the big picture. But guess what? This isn't the end of the world and that's just something I'll have to deal with if and when that happens. But in the meantime, if I can show these girls the light, they just might find their way.

Guidance is really important is the whole scheme of things. If you can influence a person to make a positive change in their life, no matter how big or small, I'd call that a job well done. So there I was, expecting my life to come crashing down around me and things ended up being ok; even better in some aspects.

Letting your emotions get the best of you can be dangerous. Taking control of them and tightening the reigns is pivotal in the race to save your emotional health. Remember, you want to be the one to walk away from any situation with your head held high. And it can be done.

HAIR OF THE DOG

I'm not quite sure what made me want to start dating again, but after the permanence of my break up set in, I suppose it was helpful to find something else to complain about. Hell, I was being asked out left and right and suddenly decided to start saying "yes".

In only a few weeks time, I'd entered several new characters into the lineup in my phonebook. Each of them was tall, good looking and successful in their field. While it may sound promising, those traits don't exactly guarantee a good guy; or even a good date, for that matter.

Jeff---Daddio. Call me selfish, but I'd never be his #1. His child and his baby's mama would always come before me. Besides, being a loving dad is one thing, but smoking a joint while your kid is napping in the other room is a different story. Don't think so. Next.

Tim---Compulsive Liar. I caught him in several silly lies and later found out that he was engaged to a beautiful blonde. Nice try. Next.

Adam---Mr. Couple. Honey, baby, sweetie…..he wanted to be part of something so badly that he didn't care who played the counterpart. I'll pass. Next.

Brendan---Motormouth. This guy shows up late with a black eye and then tells me about his recent addiction to cocaine. Great selling point, don't you think? Why me? Next.

Rob---PUNK. He just liked to push people's buttons. We got into a huge argument over the phone after he made a comment about my friend, who happened to be in a wheelchair. Needless to say, we never did have that second date. Game over. Next.

Eric---Mr. Blah. This guy was born with the personality of a shoe. Not a pump or a cute, strappy sandal or even a big old boot. Think shoe on the side of the road. And then, after an extremely long, boring afternoon, he had the audacity to ask me back to his place. Nope. Next.

Jonathan---Nancy Boy. Forget for just a moment that it probably took him an hour or two longer than me to get ready, but he showed up with a group of his friends. And guys have the nerve to talk about girls going to the bathroom together! Are you surprised that I had one polite beer and then hit the road? Get lost, pal. Next.

Matt---Foul 5-0. Looks like working those overnight shifts in the ghetto are starting to get to him. Didn't anyone ever tell him not to use the c-word in front of a lady? He brought new meaning to the word pig. Beat it. Next.

Scott---Gameboy. Here today, gone tomorrow. He'd rush right into meeting the family and then disappear for a few days. Through mutual friends, I found out that he had been in a relationship for quite a while. I wasn't into playing hide and seek and no one likes a liar. No way. Next.

Mike---Pillman. I tried my best to deal with his extremely off sense of humor. But then, he launched into his use of prescription drugs to keep his severe depression at bay. Nice topic of conversation for a first date! Are you kidding? Next.

Joe---Mr. No Clue. I wouldn't be surprised if I was this guy's first date ever. He wasn't doing a very good job with anything. He was nervous and no matter how hard I tried, I couldn't get a conversation going. We yawned in each other's faces throughout dinner and then he asked for help with the bill. Sorry. Next.

Nick---Funkdafied. This is going to sound so shallow, but this guy smelled funny. He was a nice enough guy, but if I can smell your funk from the seat next to you, I'm concerned about what's going on underneath your clothes. In fact, that's a place I'd like to never go. No thanks. Next.

Sal---Unbelievable. Nevermind that he took me to a sports bar so that he didn't have to miss his favorite TV show, it was worse than that. He was a "my body is my temple" kind of guy. He was so tormented by food and empty calories that I just had to order a bunch of fried appetizers and

Spilled Milk

eat them in front of him. Sure, he had a six pack somewhere underneath his façade, but the best part of that date was his BMW, when it dropped me off. Scram. Next.

I was exhausted after interviewing one schmuck after another. Given, I had enjoyed a few good meals, a ballgame and couple of random involuntary laughs, but ultimately I was disappointed. The one thing each of these outings had in common, was that I was the best part of it. The evidence is that each of them wanted to see me again. Pompous or not, it's true.

My short lived serial dating spree proved that all I needed was a little hair of the dog that bit me. It actually gave me a little hope and here's why: the more you try, the more likely you are to succeed. It's almost like playing the lottery. I'd been out with a number of people and didn't care for any of them. But with odds like that, it wouldn't be long before someone would come along and catch my attention.

RAISING THE BAR

Knowing what you want is quite possibly the most important quality to have as a single woman. You have your career in place, a sufficient residence and now all that's missing is the one you want to see in your spare time. How hard could that be to find?

The old saying "beggars can't be choosers" is absolutely right. However, what may be news to most is that not all single women are begging for a man's attention.

Sure, the older and wider they get, the more desperate single women tend to become. There's no denying that whatsoever. The older they get and the more afraid of dying alone they are, the more likely they are to overlook certain imperfections and inadequacies. She may not mind that he's shorter and has a bad case of halitosis, as long as he's there when she wakes up each day.

But the girls in my boat see things a little differently. The fear of growing old alone is not yet an issue for us. Why? We don't feel threatened by it because we know that if this one strikes out, there's always another batter waiting in line. In fact, that may be part of the problem. We are young, talented, intelligent and unlike generations before us, self-sufficient. Why would we settle for anything less than the ideal?

Of course we'd all like to find our match on the first try, but understand that it's not likely. That's where the process of elimination begins.

Thank god we're young and relatively well rested, because dating can be exhausting. It easily gets to the point where you've got your answers ready before they even ask the question. It's a different face asking, but in reality, you're on the same date over and over again. Single women know this routine.

Spilled Milk

It takes someone special to break the mold and really blow you away to even be considered for a second date. And most importantly, they must avoid turning you off at any point during the night to even get that far. Settling for any less than you've imagined is insulting. We've all been out with the guys who think it's ok to cop a feel right off the bat. I'd like to shake the woman's hand who first thought of the "emergency" phone call during a bad date. Thank you!

When you're out with someone new, you've got to keep your eyes peeled for red flags. Whether it's an extremely foul mouth or a noticeably quick temper, it triggers that thought in your head immediately: This guy is not coming back for round two!

I am not perfect by any means. I am outspoken, impatient and require a daily nap for the safety of those around me. I have little tolerance, rarely refill ice cube trays and have been known to snore on occasion. So who am I to judge?

I am the person who decides if this applicant stays in my life or not. That's who I am. If something about this person falls short, it's not only my right, but my responsibility to turn them away. Why would anyone spend time with another if deep down you really don't want to? You've got to want it. And if you don't; that's that.

So when the gentleman menu is in your hands, will you know what you want? Are you even aware of what there is to choose from?

According to a study performed from 1999-2002 complete with measurement evidence, the height of the average American man is 5'9". That's fine and dandy for those average sized woman out there, but vertically challenged men just don't make the cut for me. I stand 5'11" in a good pair of heels, I'm easily 6'2". Therefore, I require my suitors to stand between 6'2" and 6'5'. They're out there. Why shouldn't one of them be mine?

I often hear that my height requirement is silly. What's the problem with dating a guy shorter than you? Well, besides your average "short man's syndrome" that comes up, I'll tell you what the problem is. I spend every day of my life being bigger than everyone. When the day comes to

Kit Campbell

an end, only my man can make me feel delicate and for an Amazon like me, it's the closest thing to heaven.

We all have our own list of requirements. It has nothing to do with conceit or egotism. This is life. Believing that the population of single men out there do not have their own list is just absurd. Be smart, recognize what it is you need and want; but don't get too carried away. Just remember not to get too righteous in your decisions. He may have a thin thighs requirement up his sleeve, so compromise is always an option. It's only fair.

But I'll do you one better and skip that nonsense for the time being. Let's talk numbers just for a minute. According to the U.S. Census Bureau as of 2006, there are an estimated 1,325,000 men living in Chicago. Roughly, 1,276,000 of them are Caucasian, my personal preference. While the majority of those men are ages 18 and older, there are still quite a few exclusions. Aside from those that are younger than me by a few years or the ones that are more than ten years older inside that bracket, there's more to worry about. 220,000 of them are under the age of 5 and 280,000 of them are 65 and older. Ladies, don't scream! I realize how scary this is starting to sound. Relax. Take a deep breath.

Ok, so now we're down to 776,000 men. Forget for just a split second that Chicago is home to the biggest gay community in the Midwest, but how many of them besides that are married? Plus, there's no census that shows how many creeps, losers and weirdos that may include. I was never one for arithmetic, but it seems there isn't much to choose from.

Each one of us is hoping to land the one we've been waiting for. The one who always hopes it's you when the phone rings, who loves to make you laugh those big, loud belly laughs. He's out there. You have to believe he is. He's the one who thinks you look beautiful first thing in the morning, even after a rough night. Do not resolve to be with anyone but the right one, long term that is. You want the one who "gets you". Now all you have to do is go out and get him

ON HOLIDAY

After a deep dive back into the working world, summer was here along with tourists from all over the world. When the Taste of Chicago hits, the city becomes a circus and for once, I was ready and willing to join the madness.

It was Fourth of July weekend and after work, I met with the crew over at my favorite pub. It wasn't as busy as I had imagined and after scanning the room, we took our seats at the bar.

It wasn't long before one of the regulars asked if I'd known about the British invasion. Because I did not, I was immediately introduced to the two visiting Englishmen seated at the table behind me.

The younger one, Mike, was a boisterous blonde and it was no secret that he'd be cut off soon. His older brother, David was charming, handsome and with only a few words in that British accent, I knew I'd be rethinking my stance on meeting guys in bars.

I believe it was Chaka Khan who once said, "gone are the days of instant romance" but with all due respect, nothing could have been further from the truth. David and I had hit if off instantly and for us, the night was just getting started. It was well after midnight but how could Josh and I resist taking these boys for a little sightseeing? We danced for a while at a nearby club and laughed about it later on at an afterhours joint close by. From there, Mike was ready to pass out, so we put him in a cab and sent him back to his hotel. Josh, the remaining Brit and I took the scenic route along the river and walked back to Josh's place.

David was in awe of our great city and amazed at how warm Chicago nights could be. Apparently, he had no idea what was in store for him. He was a complete gentleman; handholding, always walking on the street side, etc. His mother must have taught him well.

Kit Campbell

By the time we got back to Josh's place and woke up his roommate, it was decided the time had come for our night to end. The first chance for David and I to be alone together came when we stepped into the elevator to leave the building. I'd be damned if I was going to push the button that would take us to the ground floor and out the door. Instead, I punched the one that carried us to the rooftop deck.

David became almost childlike with excitement to be up so high and in the middle of a skyline he'd only seen before in pictures. We talked and talked and before I knew it, his lips were touching mine.

From there, began what turned out to be my most exciting one night stand to date. He kissed me just the way I like to be kissed and his touch was electric. Soon the skyline was behind me and my face was to the stars, he wasted no time showing off his talents. I was impressed, to say the least, with his upper body strength as he held me up against the deck railing and continued. I could hear my voice echo high above the sleeping city and our summer sweat had already begun to mix. After exhausting all possibilities on the rooftop, we headed to his hotel, but not before I reciprocated a favor or two down in the mailroom.

His suite was on the seventh floor of a grand hotel on the Magnificent Mile. After kicking off my shoes and letting my clothes hit the floor, he followed me into the shower for some good, clean fun.

Now I know nothing of pheromones or scientific reason why two people are able to connect in such a way, but I'm convinced chemistry is somehow responsible. Using words like passion or intensity do not come close to describing what took place that night. We are truly the human animal. I could explain the playfulness in the shower, denote the curtains on the balcony that later came crashing down or how the sheets were stripped from the bed from being grasped so tightly, but words still cannot describe. No details could do justice to the fire we created in that room.

The sun would be up in a matter of minutes, and I chose to depart and avoid having my car towed, rather than staying with him to sleep the morning away. He politely offered me the telephone number to his room and in return I gave him my cell number. Given the circumstances, I knew I would never hear from him again and I was okay with that.

Spilled Milk

Connections like that aren't built to last. He walked me to my car which was illegally parked a few blocks away and kissed me goodbye. From there, I drove out of sight and that was the last I ever saw of David.

Later that day, I woke up wondering if I had imagined it all, but the bruises on my shoulders and hips proved that I had not. The images of our liaison would dance in my head for hours and force a devilish smile upon my face.

I don't normally answer calls from numbers I don't recognize, but was shocked and happy to hear that delightful British accent come over the line. It was David, calling to thank me for such an extraordinary time. It was his first trip to the states and one that he promised he would never forget.

Although barbaric in some of our capers, he remained a gentleman from beginning to end and I thanked him for that. I agreed that our evening was unforgettable and wished him a safe flight home. He said that it was important for me to realize that I was responsible for the best holiday he had ever experienced. And that was it. We said our goodbyes.

I had joined David on holiday and didn't even have to leave the comfort of my hometown. It was refreshing to put my concerns to rest, if only for a day or two. Perhaps that was the vacation I was so desperately in need of. I knew it would all be over before it even started and I went along for the ride anyway. No broken hearts, no sleepless nights; just a perfect memory of a story that I will never get tired of telling.

LIVING LIFE

Good girls stay at home with broken hearts. I picked that up somewhere, but have grown to disagree. I wouldn't say it's healthy to completely ignore heartache, but who's got time to embrace it? It's just that if your ex thought you were smart, gorgeous and funny, there's a good chance the rest of the world might just agree. I like those odds.

In my quest for contentment, I have discovered that opportunities arise more frequently and with higher stakes when you're flying solo. Perhaps it's as simple as approachability. But then, maybe we carry ourselves differently when we're on our own. We stand a little taller, speak a little stronger and have everyone convinced that we're capable of anything. When those around you start to take notice, is when the amazing offers come rolling in.

Let's talk shop. In the entertainment industry, you need more than to be good at what you do to get by. We set out to project an image to solidify the show we were selling. Because our program focused on love and relationships, we provided the city with a lineup that the listeners could fall in love with.

It was a simple recipe. First off there's Lee, the host of the show and the most important ingredient. His sensuous voice, universal good looks and impeccable style easily drew in the listeners. As his sidekick and producer, I brought a woman's point of view to the table, a steamy voice with a smile to match and a reason for our listeners' husbands to tune in along with them. We were attractive and available, always understanding and only a phone call away. Voila!

Hear that? It's opportunity knocking. Soon we were hosting huge events in the city and being invited to prestigious affairs. We always opted to attend these gatherings alone because if the right person raises their glass to you, the last thing you need is someone there to weigh you down. Connections were made and the doors were flying open.

Spilled Milk

Sometimes though, it seems as if there just isn't enough room for two. This is where your solitude works for you. Say a chance meeting with the tour manager of a high profile group offers you a seat on the bus. This means five days, three cities and uncensored nights like they talk about on MTV. I hardly think there would be a place for your boyfriend, or mine for that matter. There is only room for one, so will you take that seat? I did.

The stories accrued in a situation like that, easily top just another movie night at his place, where you get the pleasure of watching him fall asleep on the couch. But you're single now and there's no need to worry about leaving anyone behind. What you do have to worry about is that you've only got ten minutes to pack!

Opportunities come in many disguises and they are different for everyone. Why not work the extra hours? Impress your boss and have yours be the first name he thinks of come promotion time. In some instances, a break can come effortlessly. Just be thankful that you can accept any invitation you like, without asking for anyone's approval. Dance with whomever you please!

It's our responsibility to enjoy the freedom we've had cast upon us. This freedom encourages us to do as we wish. Besides, who wants to stay in the shadows when there's a big, bright world out there? When opportunity knocks, will you answer?

So go backstage, sleep 'til noon, smile more often and really live your life. Tomorrow comes so that yesterday can be gone. Take the chance to see and do the things you've only talked about. Life isn't always one, big party. But then, I suppose it could certainly feel like one. So why sit at home with your hair in a bun? Remember, good girls stay at home with broken hearts. But smart girls go wherever they want.

TICK TOCK

I've always tried to make it a monthly affair to have lunch with my married friends. I've known two of them since kindergarten and have always been fairly close to them. They skipped right over the singles scene and right into their happily-ever-afters. I've noticed that these types of gatherings are necessary to maintain friendships after marriage comes into play. They married great guys, and I'm happy for them both; but the truth is, wanting to gossip over a fattening lunch was basically the only thing we had in common anymore.

They talked about recipes they were trying out on their husbands, I talked about the chic restaurants I'd been taken to on dates. They spoke of retirement plans, I spoke of weekend trips to Mexico. They asked me how it was going with that guy I was dating, I asked them which one.

I remember the first time they met Perry. They too were convinced that he was the one for me. They couldn't wait to start making big plans for our future. They wondered what color my bridesmaids would be wearing and I wondered if he would ever officially ask me.

Well, now we know the answer to that question! It's funny, because when Perry left, the girls didn't know quite how to handle it either. They didn't see it happening, and neither did I. It was like they were afraid to come in contact with me for a while, which was probably all for the best. Eventually, though, they made their reappearances.

They conditioned me early on, to believe that my life was much more exciting than theirs. While it took some time for me to realize that they were right, when said in that sympathetic, "I'm married, you're not" tone, you get the message loud and clear. I was getting the pity talk from my friends. They focused on my career and on my social life, leaving the concept of finding love again, in the dust. I know deep down they have always wanted the best for me, but weren't very talented in letting it show. Either that, or I was taking things entirely too personally. But

Spilled Milk

who's to blame? Was it the married girls calling attention to the fact that I was the only single one? Or was I segregating myself and not even knowing it?

The answer was plain to see as the subject of pregnancy came up during one of our lunches. The girls had decided they were ready to start "trying" in that department. It was almost amusing, as the rest of us have always been "trying not to" for so long.

Don't get me wrong, I want to have kids more than anyone would ever suspect. I imagine myself bringing up a big family; I've always had my mind set on four. But because the girls have a head start by being married, my remarks in the conversation weren't taken very seriously. Again, they used my career as an excuse to focus on something other than family.

Meanwhile, I started to think that this was an incredibly inappropriate conversation while I was sitting at the table, if they didn't want my input on the topic. It got to the point where the girls were reserving names for their future children, but didn't care much about the names I had picked out. Why? It must have been a ridiculous idea for me to even have names picked out, right? It's not like every girl alive doesn't have them picked out by the time she's ten! I left that lunch feeling a little down on myself. For the first time, I was started to get nervous that I was always going to be the single friend. And worse, I worried that the day would never come when someone would call me "mom".

Was my career getting in the way of what I envisioned as my happily ever after? Or was that just a copout to make me feel better about being alone? Sure, I wanted to be a wife, but even more, I wanted to a mom. Why wasn't this happening to me the way it was happening to them? Was I missing something?

Later on that evening I was packing for an upcoming vacation, but realized that something was missing. I was scheduled to have my monthly visitor almost a week prior and it skipped my mind until that moment. I had it figured out to be wrapping up just in time for my road trip, but it never showed up in the first place.

I waited two more days to be sure that I wasn't creating a stressful situation for no reason. Still, nothing was happening. I had been pretty regular for quite some time and always use protection, so I was starting to get concerned. I drove to my cousin's house, where she had a pregnancy test waiting for me. Her mother works at a fertility clinic and she had one extra laying around, just in case. We decided it was best to get right to it.

We must have read the directions ten times, but it didn't make the situation any better for us. The answer became painfully clear, when both of those damn purple dots showed up on the display. Pregnant.

Now I know what it feels like to have a panic attack. My blood went rushing to my head and I could feel my heart beating in my throat, hear it in my ears. There were so many questions pounding in my head all at once and as surprising as it may seem, I was thinking so clearly.

I wasn't worried about how I was going to take care of a baby. I wasn't concerned about the financial aspect of raising a child or how it might affect my career. I didn't mind that everything I planned for myself would have to be put on hold in order to make my child my first priority.

Instead, I worried about how I was going to explain this to everyone. Where would I begin? It was bad enough that this was a product of a single night of passion with a stranger, but we'll take it one step farther that now he's an ocean away and no, there's no way I can get a hold of him. I wouldn't even know where to begin trying to track him down. Should I even bother?

Suddenly, there was no filter between what I was thinking and what I was saying. I was becoming hysterical. Every thought from my brain was spilling from my lips and nothing could make it stop. Was this really happening? Would I have to tell everyone how this happened? That I met him in a bar? That we went back to his hotel? That he lives in London? That I have no way of contacting him at all? That I brought this on myself? What am I going to do? What am I going to do?

My brain was replaying a conversation I once had with Perry regarding pregnancy. He told me that if we found out that I had become

Spilled Milk

pregnant, the first thing he would do is take me to the courthouse and marry me. Why couldn't a surprise like this happen while we were together, rather than being the result of some wild one nighter? Wait.

Wait. We used a condom. This can't be right. We were careful, weren't we? Think, Kit. Oh, god. It was all coming back to me now. The shower. Oh, god; that one that broke later on in the bed. Oh, god. This can't be happening.

We hopped in the car and headed to the closest 24 hour pharmacy and picked up another test. I wanted to be damn sure of this, before I sat down and told my mom what was going on. Within ten minutes we were back at her place, in the bathroom. I took the test and immediately saw that wretched shade of purple again.

I could barely keep my balance and sat down on the edge of the tub. I tried to call for my cousin but when I opened my mouth, no sound came out. She was calling my name but I couldn't answer her. She came in and brought the test into her sight. She smiled and showed it to me. Not pregnant.

But I saw it. Only a minute before it was purple, I knew it. But she showed it to me again, and it said I wasn't pregnant. Which one of these am I supposed to believe? I don't need this. I can't do this right now. I have the life everyone wants. I'm supposed to be leaving on vacation tomorrow. I'm supposed to be drinking early in the morning down on the beach like a rock star. I'm not supposed to be the girl who got pregnant by some guy that she'll never see again.

I wanted to cry, but my entire body wasn't working anymore. I needed to go home. I needed to put this day to an end. My cousin assured me that no matter what the case may be, that we would figure something out. I'm not even sure that I fell completely asleep that night. I remember being somewhere between asleep and awake, worrying about what I was going to do. Time never went by so slowly.

When I finally had the courage to get out of bed in the morning to use the bathroom, a comforting discovery took place. My visitor had arrived; better late than never. I can't say I have ever been as relieved as I was at that moment. Funny, how quickly I was able to regain control of

Kit Campbell

my life. The night before I was completely hysterical and now I was calm and cool. That was a close one.

Nothing like a good old fashioned pregnancy scare to rattle your brain, right? It really made me think, though. I thought I wanted a baby as much as my married friends, but while I thought I had one growing inside me, it wasn't such a colorful thought. It was instead very frightening and nerve wrecking at this point in my life. Eventually, yes; I want to have to have children. I want lots and lots of them. But I also want someone there to share it with me. I want my family and friends to congratulate my man and I on our pregnancy, not wonder who the father is. Believe me, I still want them; just not right now. Not like this.

Had a seed been planted during that delightful British invasion, everything would have been a lot different. I'm convinced I would have stepped up to the plate, taken responsibility and hit a homerun. But luckily, that's not what happened. And now I have the luxury of foresight.

So the way I see it, this is all about preparation. Just like most women, I want things to go in order. First comes love, then comes marriage, then comes the baby in the baby carriage. Isn't that the way we always planned it?

LOVE OR MONEY

The term "gold-digger" is not exactly a new addition to our vocabulary. It's been around for ages, but is used more frequently now than ever before. Today's men are so quick to brand a woman with that label, so what's the harm in checking it out? It's no different than a dress; try it on and see if it fits.

My experience in spending time with the other half was not only brief was completely unexpected. It started with an afternoon of intoxication at a ballgame. It seemed to me that we'd be up for an exciting night because after the game, we skipped jumping on the train and stepped into a limousine instead.

The girl I went to the game with, ran into an old co-worker, who invited us to join the party. From what I was told, Betty was tagged as a gold-digger from day one. She was a beautiful Polish import; thin and blonde with a sassy personality. She was a sweet gal, but not exactly the brightest crayon in the box. Betty was known for dating guys as old as our parents and had no problem letting them pick up the tab. No stranger to heartache, she was tired of trying to make relationships work. She was ready for love to work for her. She was draped in high fashion, her apartment was top shelf and from where Betty was standing, she was now in the land of opportunities.

When I crawled into the first vacant spot in the limo, I immediately knew what was going on. There were four of us young ladies and conveniently four, much older men, joining us. There's nothing like alcohol to impair judgment, so I stayed.

The fourth girl in the car was a china doll with a bite like a snake. Just like those mail order brides you see in the movies, she was on the arm of a man at least thirty years her elder and had a handbag that probably cost more than my car. As far as gold-diggers go, this girl was a professional.

Kit Campbell

We arrived at a lounge near Greektown and I couldn't believe my eyes when I saw one of the men pay the maitre'd to clear out the entire south end of the club so our group could have some privacy.

I felt extraordinarily underdressed in my tank top and ponytail when the staff started waiting on us hand and foot. Shortly after we'd taken our seats, the group had doubled in size.

It was then that the secret was out. Not only was I in the company of a handful of professional gold-digger's, but a group of prominent Illinois politicians, including but not limited to three (married) mayors of Chicago's surrounding suburbs.

And then there was the one they called The Million Dollar Man. He was by far the youngest guy in the bunch. I was told he was in his late twenties, although it looked a little more like he was pushing forty. The Million Dollar Man was obnoxious and loud, not to mention aggravating the hell out of me by repeatedly showing me his ten pound watch that was covered in diamonds. I'd been drinking all day, so my snide comments weren't exactly few and far between. Besides, I've never been one to keep my opinions or smart remarks to myself. He must have thought that my bad attitude was part of my charm because wouldn't you just know it? He had a thing for yours truly.

Now I understood early on that there were even numbers of men and women in our section. But I didn't realize how severe the situation was until the Million Dollar Man tried putting his million dollar hands between my blue collar knees. He'd been slightly handsy earlier on, but I thought I had corrected that. Didn't he see that I wasn't like these other girls? You'd think a man who flaunts a watch like that would recognize a purse from Target in no time! With a swift elbow to his jaw, he learned how girls from my neighborhood justify that kind of behavior.

His response? "Finally you brought me one with some fire!" It was then that I realized I wasn't there by chance. I was sucked into meeting a would-be sugar daddy by a friend of a friend and didn't even know it until I was already in his clutches.

Perhaps it was the consummation that made my stomach turn. Perhaps it was the whiskey I had been choking down. Either way, I was

Spilled Milk

ready to leave and at that hour, my only option was catching a ride home in the limo.

I was aggravated beyond words that I allowed myself to be put in such a situation. To some, this could have been, literally, a golden opportunity. It's not every day that an heir to millions wants your company, but I declined immediately.

After being unable to reckon with his growing advances, I had no choice but to let my nausea show. What a mess I made in the back of that car! He pleaded with me to use a bag, to let him roll down the window, give him a minute so the driver could pull over. But it was no use. I opted to make myself as unappealing as possible and sticking it to him at the same time. After all, he was the Million Dollar Man; he could afford to have his Lincoln reupholstered!

Even in my drunken stupor, it was all very apparent to me. Money doesn't have any meaning to me if it comes along with a massive lack of respect. I don't need a seven hundred dollar handbag and I probably never will. What I need is someone to take care of me, emotionally, not financially.

Now believe me, I'm not knocking girls like Betty. If you can forego your emotions and be happy enough with the cash, then more power to you! I pray the day never arrives when I am so jaded with love that the closest thing to making me happy is an old man with a foul mouth and a fat wallet. If it works for both people, involved, then by all means, carry on.

But it just wouldn't work for me. You can't say I didn't entertain the idea, but the shoe just didn't fit. I suppose I'll hold out for the right one, even if all is has to offer me is his heart. Well, that and a killer smile. Anything on top of that is just an added bonus. Once you have his heart, that's when you've really hit the jackpot. And I guess in order to win, you've got to play the game. Knowing my luck, I'll probably fall for someone who drives a station wagon.

37

ERROR

Just leave it to me to have the CD player in my car break the day I have to take a long drive. I took an evening off early in July, to spend some time with a dapper young man, whose unfortunate nickname was Shabby. His alias barely did him justice, as I was completely drawn to him. He was tall, dark and handsome with intelligence and a quick wit. Believe it or not, he had me hooked the first night.

He lived in a brick two flat on the city's far north side, nearly an hour from me. He lived only a few blocks from the lake, so I offered to drive up to his neighborhood, so that we could pass time together at the beach.

I was already running late for our first date when I realized that the CD player in my car wasn't working. I was dangerously close to throwing a tantrum. I tried to feed it a disc, but it was spit out immediately. Not only would it not accept my music, but it made a loud, buzzing sound and the display screen read, "ERROR". So there I was, stuck in rush hour traffic on Lake Shore Drive, listening to annoying afternoon radio jocks, over that incessant buzzing.

I forgot all about my technical difficulties once we were together. I forgot about a lot of things when we were together. This was the first time in a long time that I relished my time with someone. After a few sleepovers, we decided to go ahead and start a relationship.

It all happened so fast, one minute I was crying for someone, the next I was staying up all night talking to my new flame. You know those types of talks when you first start to fall for someone; the kind that last four or five hours at a time and when the battery on your cell starts to die, you're still not ready to say goodnight. Things were looking up for me.

That is, until he decided to come clean. Apparently, he had a girlfriend for the first few weeks of our relationship. I'm not sure where

Spilled Milk

he found time to speak with her because he was engulfed with me. But they always find a way, don't they? His story was that he was trying to let her down gently after the day he met me. Plus the reason he didn't tell me that he was taken was that he didn't want me to lose interest. How typical.

I bawled him out for lying to me. I hate liars. I thought he knew that. He was extremely apologetic and I had to give him credit for finally being honest with me. He never had to tell me the truth about his status when we met, so I approved of him doing so. He seemed so sincere when he told me that he was just doing what he had to do, to be with me. It was music to my ears when he explained that he couldn't allow me to get away from him. He thought if he didn't do everything in his power to be with me, that he would regret it for the rest of his life. After hearing all of that, how could I let him go? I cared about him so much already, that I gave him the second chance I felt he deserved.

And so we continued on. I spent every day off with him and he stayed up all night talking to me on the phone when I had to work an overnight shift. He cooked me dinners and sent me flowers. Hell, he wanted to book me for a vacation with him next summer! For a minute there, I really thought we were going somewhere.

But then, the left side of my brain started to mess with me. When I'd find myself missing Shabby, I started to feel guilty that I wasn't missing Perry as much anymore. Had I found a replacement? Was I an awful person for doing so or had he already replaced me as well? It wasn't anything I wanted to focus on. Things were going well between Shabby and I; the last thing I wanted to do was ruin it.

I completely cared for him. We were seemingly mad about each other from the beginning, so why not continue? Speaking of which, that damn CD player in my car was persistently buzzing and showing ERROR. Since Shabby was a tech guy, he offered to take a look at it. When he couldn't figure it out, we took it to a car stereo shop to have it looked at. The guys were stumped, but were quick to offer me a deal on a hot new system. Shabby had just helped me pick out a new digital camera for myself that was going to set me back several hundred dollars.

Kit Campbell

So the system would have to wait. I would be forced to see that screen blink ERROR for at least another paycheck or two.

I went against everything my Southside upbringing stands for, when Shabby took me to my first Cubs game. I made it painfully clear to him that I would remain a White Sox fan for life, but agreed to go with him because he wanted to introduce me to his family. The next thing I knew, his friends were patting him on the back and telling him not to screw this one up. His sister even invited me to her birthday party and we became quite the couple.

I'm not even sure why it all went to hell so fast. Perhaps it was because my blindness to all the red flags finally came to an end. I started to notice things that were really bothersome to me. He would promise and never deliver. The phone calls started to become few and far between, except of course right before a sleepover and for when we had plans and he needed me on his arm. He was becoming noticeably distant and the time came for us to have a little talk.

His predictable defense was that he was really busy, but I've heard all that before. Besides, I stand by the notion that if someone is important to you, they will find two minutes to reach out to you. Because let's face it, that's all it really takes. He swore up and down the wall that he thought about me all day and would make the effort to change for the better. Strike two, but we pressed on. After all, I was crazy about him and his family was crazy about me. You can't give up that easy.

Then came the afternoon that I stopped by his place and noticed his hockey jersey on the floor. Now it was late August and his apartment felt like a sauna, so I wondered why this heavy thing was on the floor. My curiosity went wild, mostly because that was what I slept in every time I spent the night. My paranoia kicked in and I worried that he was sharing his bed with someone else.

To presume such a thing was apprehensive, I'm sure. But a few years back, I dated a guy from Las Vegas who moved to Chicago to take care of his grandmother. We were in his basement one night and I thought I saw a black thong on the laundry room floor. While it was none of my business, I worried that he was seeing someone else and seeing her often enough that she felt comfortable leaving without her panties. The only

40

Spilled Milk

other explanation was that it belonged to his 89 year old grandmother, which was not only disturbing, but highly unlikely. I never did ask him about it. But I didn't really need to, seeing as only two weeks later, he left me for his ex. Fine; lesson learned. Keep your eye out for red flags.

So there I was, staring down at that jersey with this on my mind. I picked it up and hung it on the chair next to the bed. He quickly scooped it up and threw it in the hamper. Was he nervous or just tidy? Did I look insecure? Was I becoming all the things I thought I wasn't? I ignored it and chose to enjoy my time with him instead.

Once again, I started noticing the distance again. After a couple of date cancellations, I really started getting annoyed. No longer was I worried, I was fed up.

While we will never forget how horrible it was for the Gulf Coast to endure Hurricane Katrina and her aftermath, I felt like I was the only girl in the Midwest to experience her fury. Shabby had a close friend who lived in New Orleans and without thinking it through or mentioning it to me, he offered the southerner a place to stay while the city was rebuilt. He regretted it instantly, when his friend gratefully accepted and drove to Chicago the next day.

He was hesitant to tell me what he'd done and I certainly wasn't pleased to hear it, but this was the situation we found ourselves in. We already had a problem finding time to see each other and it wouldn't be any easier with a new roommate from out of town. I was just waiting for the other shoe to drop and sure enough, it did. His new roommate was not only a close friend, she was a woman; a woman he used to date.

That was when I hit the ceiling. How was he supposed to build a relationship with me when he was living with his ex? Are you kidding me? He promised that the situation would be extremely temporary and like a fool, I went along with it. Wow. See how caring for someone can make those red flags just disappear?

I took a phone call from my grandmother that week and she casually asked me how things were going with Shabby. When I told her that it wasn't going very well lately, she said she had a feeling it was heading

Kit Campbell

down the drain. I wondered why, seeing as the two of them had never met, but brushed it off.

When Shabby's ex arrived in Chicago, I went an entire week without hearing from him. I was at the point where I thought he would never call again. But sure enough, Saturday night rolls around and he expects me to spend the night.

I realize now that trying to break it off over the phone wasn't appropriate, but I couldn't take it anymore. I couldn't take wondering whether or not I would hear from him or worrying what was going on now that Shabby and his ex were sleeping under the same roof. It was making me crazy and I had to put a stop to it.

It didn't go well at all. He showed a side of himself that I had never seen or heard before. He starting swearing and name-calling; telling me how selfish I was for wanting his attention this week. Attempting to talk through anything at this point was futile. Though I realized there were at least 50 miles between us while we were arguing, I was slightly frightened. Never have I angered someone like that before. The most horrible things were spilling out of his mouth and I couldn't believe he was speaking to me this way. Shabby was my first spark of hope that I would fall in love again but his lack of attention and display of rage quickly extinguished it. He screamed a few more hateful words and hung up the phone.

I don't know what happened after that. I was holding back the tears because I was entirely too furious to let them show. I grabbed the vase of flowers that he sent to my office the week prior, jumped in my car and headed to his house. I pictured myself smashing the vase against his front door or on the windshield of his car, as if that would make the situation better.

I called my friend, Madison to bring her up to speed, plus I needed her female backup. I had always prided myself on not being a crazy woman, and Maddy reminded me of that. She said if I actually drove to Shabby's place to cause a scene that I would be behaving like a crazy woman. Besides, if he was that volatile over the phone, imagine his reaction when I showed up at his door. She was completely right. I don't know what came over me and thank god she was there to snap me out of it.

Spilled Milk

I continued my ride into the city and planned to arrive at work a little early. But I knew I needed some hateful, angry music to help me cope during my drive. I grabbed my "Pretty Hate Machine" CD and pushed it into the CD player. There's nothing like some good old Nine Inch Nails to help ease the pain. It wasn't until track one was almost over, that I realized my broken CD player was working just fine. It was no longer buzzing and the display didn't read "ERROR".

And there you have it. Maybe while I was busy ignoring all the other red flags, I had one spelled out for me the whole time. ERROR. How haunting that it started the first day we were together and came to a halt the day we fell apart. It was at that very moment, I knew that I had made the right decision to end it.

But the story doesn't end there. Not one week later, he had the audacity to bring his new girlfriend to a ritzy restaurant downtown, knowing full well that my friend, Josh, runs the place and would report it back to me. So not only did Shabby turn out to be a total creep, but a star on the front page of the paper as well. I should probably avoid any slander charges; seeing as he hasn't exactly been convicted yet.

Is there a lesson here? Sure. Love can blind you. But it doesn't have to make you deaf and dumb, too. Be aware of your situation and choose carefully the things you disregard. You can only overlook so many things. Furthermore, the last thing you want to do is make a grave ERROR.

WHAT ABOUT YOUR FRIENDS?

Most people think they have the greatest friends in the world. I am no exception to the rule. When you're in a relationship with someone, it's important not to neglect your friends. Granted, when you're in love, it feels like when the two of you are together, you don't need anyone else. But if and when your lover bails on you, it's your friends who will pick you up and dust you off. They'll be armed with a new pair of heels and the hottest lip color on the market. They'll be generous with hugs and carry a bag of M&M's in case of emergency.

Candy can be so helpful. It's become common knowledge that chocolate provides serotonin, a chemical which stimulates mood lifting agents in the brain. But post-Perry, I got the message loud and clear when my cousin bought me an oversized confectionary pacifier: cry if you must, but we're not staying in. She fielded the majority of my tears and even more so found a way to turn off the waterworks altogether. I knew I could use her shoulder to cry on, but what's better is that once we were together, I didn't feel much like crying anymore. I don't know what I'd do without her.

If one of my friends truly embraced my newfound single status, it was Madison. Tall and blonde, she often found herself in my boat. She was talented, clever and easy on the eyes, but couldn't get a break when it came to finding a good guy.

Even as long as my most recent relationships had lasted, Maddy never did meet any of my suitors. We had kept in touch, but didn't have our nights out like we used to. How could we? The way we used to command the room, was not suitable behavior for anyone in a relationship. But to my surprise, she was right there waiting to take me under her wing when it all ended.

If the term "partner in crime" was ever relevant, it was born between Maddy and I. She was the Thelma to my Louise. She was the first to

Spilled Milk

remind me of how fabulous I was and told me how much the scene had missed me while I was gone. Our soundtrack was on repeat, the sound of the echoing whistles of men and soon it seemed that it wasn't so bad to be back after all.

And then there's the token gay guy. I met Josh when I was seventeen and still hanging out in coffee shops. He has been the very essence of a gentleman since day one. Josh and I treated ourselves to lavish dates all the time. He always opens doors and walks on the street side, not to mention, there has never been a shortage of flowers in my life. How lucky I am to have the luxury of an upscale night on the town with a handsome man who has zero interest in getting in my drawers! It's an ideal arrangement. No pressure, plenty of laughs and nothing but fun.

Finally let's consider the healing power of touch. Did you know that massage has been proven to help alleviate symptoms of depression? While it's far too simplistic to say that depression can be cured by massage, there is truth in the high value of therapeutic touch. I could not agree more.

My longtime friend, Joe has always been very helpful in that capacity. He's no massage therapist, but his touch is truly healing. While we never kept very close contact during my relationships, Joe was more than happy to reappear after a breakup. While we've relished some carnal times together, our situation wasn't always sexual. Sometimes we'd just take naps together or fall asleep in front of the TV together. Having that closeness in the evenings was so helpful. I'd give him a backrub, he'd play with my hair. Always touching and always feeling a little better. I do believe in the healing power of touch.

I have been fortunate enough to keep a solid group of friends to catch me when I fall. Not a one of them griped about the time I was away because they were just happy to have me back. For that, I am extremely grateful. It would have been easy for them to forget about me, because while I was wrapped up in my romance, it appeared I had forgotten all about them. I have been blessed with the safety net they have supplied me with over the years and I would do anything for them.

Honestly, my friends were providing me with almost anything that a man could. I had my confidant, someone to party with until all hours,

Kit Campbell

never ending date nights and someone to wake up with. Exactly what was I missing? After everything they had done for me, it started to feel like I wasn't missing out on much at all.

If you can get yourself a couple of really good friends, then you've got it made. Everyone needs someone they can talk to and trust, who is caring and reliable. You may not see them as much as you'd like, but knowing they will be around when you need them brings contentment.

Never leave them out in the cold and always match what they bring to the table. Life's rollercoaster isn't slowing down. There are twists and turns; some of it we like, and some of it we don't. Just be thankful for that person seated next to you, no matter who it might be. Scream with them and laugh with them. Hopefully, at the end, someone will be there to hear you say, "damn, that was one hell of a ride".

HERE WE GO AGAIN

Every autumn I worry because winter is just around the corner and I know that as soon as the skies get gray, it will be a long, cold time before I see the sun again. With the way things were going, it appeared that I'd be facing this dreadful season alone.

I'd been chatting with a fellow named Charlie for a few weeks and when the time came for the first date, I finally felt some excitement again. He picked me up at my front door with a bouquet of sunflowers, with a string carrying a Dr. Pepper Chap stick, the only thing I'd ever smuggle with me on a deserted island. Wow. This guy actually pays attention, even when I was rambling about the unimportant.

He took me to a punk rock roller derby at Congress Theater and then off to a tiny railcar diner where we fed the jukebox and had our first dance. After walking me to the door and sending me off with a goodnight kiss, I was actually shaking with excitement. While gushing to my brother about my evening, I received a text message from Maddy, asking how it went. Six words told her the story: I think I'm in love again.

Two days later he invited me over to his place up north and cooked dinner for me. Soon it was ice skating, museums, concerts and pricey dinners. We couldn't seem to get enough of each other.

Before I knew it, Christmas was upon us. Charlie hosted a two day event for the two of us, picking out a tree and decorating it, followed by takeout and some time under the covers. He fit right in with my family, surviving yet another insane holiday at my parents' house and showering me with thoughtful, romantic gifts.

I have never in all my life been treated so well, so it was no wonder that winter didn't bother me so much this year. Why would it? I felt the sun every time I heard his voice, saw his face and woke up next to him. And that was it. We were in love.

Kit Campbell

For New Year's Eve, we got home from a party just in time to have a private countdown back at his place. At the stroke of midnight, we kissed just like they do in the movies. I couldn't believe my eyes when he pulled out a tiny, blue box from his pocket. The ring he slid on my finger made many promises. While it was not a proposal, I did feel what it's like to be so happy you could cry. I was trembling while he was standing there, promising me his loyalty and his friendship, but above all his love for me. He recognized my faith in him and promised he would never let me down.

I knew I was deeply in love with Charlie when I started offering to cook for him. I hate cooking. I really do, but I was so eager to please him and that was a feeling I didn't have in a long time. I would have done anything to put a smile on his face, because that's what he did for me every day.

I couldn't have been happier. Did I say that already? Does it matter? I couldn't have been happier. I never thought I was going to feel like that again. Was this really happening? Yes. And I knew it to be true every time I found flowers on my windshield, got a card in the mail and especially when he would stop me randomly and say, "Seriously, Kit, thank you for coming into my life".

After my family and friends gave their seal of approval, Maddy asked me, hypothetically, what I would do if he wanted to go to the courthouse and get married tomorrow. My answer would be simple: "Would you like me to drive?" Knowing Charlie, a courthouse wedding would never do. And I knew that because he had been jilted only a year prior. He was left out in the cold only two weeks before that long walk down the aisle. It was a touchy subject for him and as long as he swore it would never affect our relationship, it was to me, as though it had never happened.

Falling in love again wasn't supposed to be easy for either one of us, but it certainly turned out that way. Whether it was swing dancing at his favorite dive or rubbing elbows with millionaires at my company functions, we were always together. And we were happy.

Don't get me wrong, we didn't paint the town every night. Often we would stay in and cook dinner together, have indoor fixer upper

Spilled Milk

projects or sometimes just stay in bed for days at a time. He wanted me with him all the time and invited me to start keeping my things there so that I never had to leave. In no time, we turned that little one bedroom apartment into a place that we both knew, really felt like home.

This was it. I found the one that I would stay with. He was the one who always thought I was beautiful, who was constantly making me laugh and who had trouble sleeping when I wasn't there. He was responsible for my complete happiness.

The days were getting warmer, but it didn't matter. There was a cold front moving in and no one could have seen it coming.

TOO GOOD

When you're on top of the world, there's only one place to go and that's down. My career was skyrocketing and I had finally found the man of my dreams. Everything in my life had fallen into place, but it's amazing how quickly things can take a turn for the worse.

I went into work early that day for a programming meeting and was let go earlier than I had expected. It seemed our new program director had recommended yet another format change for our station, but my partner and I were unable to dodge the bullet this time. Apparently, the show we were running would not fit in with the new format and it was decided that our program would be taken off the air.

There were no thank yous for our years of dedication, nor was there any compensation for the ratings we upheld to keep that station going. I was escorted to the door and asked one last thing: "Would you like to make an appointment to pick up your things? Or should I send a messenger to drop them off?"

That's just the nature of the business I have chosen. One minute, everyone loves you and the next, no one wants to make eye contact. There are rarely any pleasant goodbyes and I turned to the one person I could count on to get me through this: Charlie. It was such horrible news, but he played it so cool. He told me everything I needed to hear at that moment. I'd find another gig, a better one. And he took pride in offering to take care of me until that day arrived.

Financially, there was no immediate danger. Human resources ended up providing me with a hefty severance package, so I had time to plot my next move. All I needed was his reassuring eyes and a sympathetic ear, things I was certain he could supply. However, Charlie was unable to accommodate. In the days that followed, he began to withdraw from me. He was working a three day stretch at the firehouse, but his calls

Spilled Milk

were few and brief. I wouldn't call it woman's intuition, because only a fool wouldn't be able to tell that something was wrong.

It should have been no surprise to me that he was prepared to break up by the end of the week, but it shocked the hell out of me. Why were we breaking up? Everything was going so well. What happened? Three days ago, Charlie couldn't imagine his life without me and now he just couldn't handle it anymore? This is not happening!

He was throwing himself a pity party, explaining that he wasn't ready to be so serious and how I should understand that because he had been scarred in the past. I thought to myself, you want to talk about scars? Let's talk about lost loves. Or better yet, let's talk about real scars, things that never really go away. I've got plenty of them, you crybaby. But I didn't launch into a counter attack. Instead, I listened.

He just kept crying and telling me how sorry he was. He was compelled to leave, although he was worried he was making the biggest mistake of his life. Where have I heard that before? I tried to reason with him, but it was no good. To top it all off, this was happening over the phone. He couldn't even face me.

When he was ready to throw in the towel, I just couldn't believe it. Maybe I didn't want to. I couldn't understand what had gone wrong. We were so in love and he told me when I lost my job that he would love me come hell or high water. Seeing as neither had come up yet, I couldn't let him go that easy. I knew from my past that it's futile to attempt to hold on after separation is on the chopping block. But I loved him so much and wasn't giving up without a fight.

I drove up to his place early the next morning for a little face to face. My heart shattered when I walked in and saw that he'd already boxed up all of my things. He couldn't even look me in the eye and we barely spoke. It was so uncomfortable and I couldn't allow it to happen that way.   I took his hand and pulled him toward me. His icy demeanor melted away when we touched and he fell to pieces in my arms. He was sobbing and kept apologizing. I told him that if what he was doing made him feel so bad, maybe he shouldn't be doing it. Whatever the problem is, it can't be so bad that we can't talk about it. I love you. I love you. I love you. Please don't do this.

Kit Campbell

After a long talk in each other's arms and tears from the both of us, it was decided that we would hang in there, give it some time. He seemingly needed some time to clear his head, so I did what anyone else would do: I booked a long weekend in Cancun. Surely by the time I got back to the states he would realize how much he loved me and needed me in his life.

I heard from him once after I arrived back in Chicago. Apparently, the only thing he needed was the peace of mind that I was home safe, because that was our final pleasant phone call. It seemed while we were apart, he'd made an absolute decision to end our relationship permanently. There was no final meeting and no long goodbye, just an email that closed with "please let this be the end no matter how hard it may be".

My car was filled with boxes I had no strength to unpack. I was out of work, out of love and damn near out of my mind. Again, my brain was filling up with questions that I'd never have the answers to. Or would I?

The only window into his life was his precious email account, the organized gateway to a majority of his social gatherings. Would I betray his trust and snoop around? You're damn right. I was on a quest to get the answers I deserved. Nothing could have prepared me for what I would find.

It appeared that my knight in shining armor was actually a wolf in sheep's clothing. I found pictures of Charlie with another woman in his arms and correspondence between the two of them. Their letters were intimate and heartbreaking to read, all of which ended in, "I love you".

It was then that I realized why he was crying. He didn't feel sadness, he felt sorry, obviously for something he had done wrong. I remembered him telling me that he valued my integrity and that's why he just couldn't stay.

Integrity: I had plenty, he undeniably, had none. The further I looked into his personal accounts, the more dreaded proof I found. I'll never know how he kept up with so many other women while we were together, but somehow he managed. Sure, there were a few he "loved",

Spilled Milk

but what's worse is that there were more lined up and waiting that he didn't seem to care for at all.

There were provocative pictures from women, accompanied by foul messages. It was so hurtful but I became addicted to it anyway. I couldn't stop exploring and soon found myself tangled in his web. I'll never understand how he could have kept so many secrets, but that didn't matter anymore. Charlie was not who I thought he was. Learning the truth is what hurt the most. I fell in love with one big, convincing lie. He was the epitome of "too good to be true".

So there I was at rock bottom. My life had fallen to pieces in a matter of days and in both cases there was no going back. Where would I go? What would I do? The only thing I knew at that moment was that once you're down so low, there's only one way to go and that's up.

MAD NOT SAD

By definition, energy is a conserved quality. It is neither created nor destroyed, only transferred. It's one of those tidbits all of us learned in sixth grade science, but something your average person considers useless information.

That is, until you find yourself having a hard time getting out of bed in the morning. Considering the sad circumstances I was forced to deal with, like many others, I often felt like I was ready to throw in the towel. My sadness sat heavy on my chest at all times. I had no appetite whatsoever and little interest in seeing or speaking to anyone. My lethal stash of meds was quickly depleting and I was drained of the hunger to start each day.

Realizing that I was ready to give up was one of the scariest things I've been faced with. Honestly concluding that I had reached a point when I didn't even want to try anymore was a horrible feeling. But believing that hope was gone, just didn't sound like me. I had started to become someone else. I didn't have my beloved career to distract me anymore and had nothing else to focus on. With my last ounce of energy, I refused to allow my sadness to paralyze me any further. I was sick and tired of being sick and tired. That's when I heard something I won't soon forget.

Be mad, not sad. My mother is a genius. It was simple and made so much sense. Anger provides fuel that you can feed on. What is it about being mad that dispenses such energy? It gave me the strength to shift my focus from deep sadness to pure anger. Now I'd have something else to concentrate on. No longer would I stay in bed, worried about yesterday or crying because I'd been so deceived. No way; I was mad.

I was mad about so many things. Immediately it was because of his lies in the first place. Then I got to thinking even more. How dare you?

Spilled Milk

How dare you do this to me only days after my devastating lay off? What a stand up guy!

He should have won an Oscar for his performance. After all that blubbering while he was breaking up with me, he had girls lined up and waiting for me to get out of the way. The more I thought about it, the angrier I became. I was full throttle and my newfound energy was the driving force.

This was a guy who was constantly proclaiming his love for me to everyone in my world and then, without warning, breaks up with me over the phone! You have got to be kidding me! Was I really going to sit around and cry over such a spineless, selfish, waste of space? I think not: energy transfer complete.

It was no surprise to me that his reappearance would take place, sooner or later. It wasn't long before I was getting text messages and emails from him trying to keep tabs on me. Each message would contain one of his patented, "side notes".

"Just wanted to see what you were up to. Side note: you're beautiful."

"How are things going? Side note: I miss you."

But I wouldn't fall for it like I did before. I wasn't the wreck he walked away from anymore. Poor thing didn't even see it coming. Side note: he's an idiot. He never even knew that I'd discovered all his dirty little secrets.

I was surrounded by an energy that boasted strength and demanded respect. Don't send me emails. If you've got something to say, call me up and say it. If you need to see me, get a plan and present it for my consideration. Until then, stop wasting my time.

I've spent enough time on my knees thank you very much. If anyone were to come crawling back, it would have to be him. I remember draining myself by trying to hold on and now it was his turn. My strength was back and there was no way in hell that I was going to let it slip away.

Kit Campbell

The energy I discovered was not created, it was there all along. All I needed was to dig deep and find it. From there, the transfer was easy and instrumental in putting myself back on the right track. Who says science is for nerds? Kudos to Bill Nye the Science Guy! Science *does* rule.

YOU SO CRAZY

Hell hath no fury like a woman scorned. Ain't that the truth? Everyone worries about what a woman is capable of once she's been burned. We've all seen Fatal Attraction. It's the fear of every man and the rage that every woman pretends she's never felt before.

It just seems so crazy to set your sights on ruining a guy's life simply because he happened to treat you like dirt. Or does it make sense? Perhaps he needs to get what's coming to him.

Now maybe it's where I grew up or maybe it's like this everywhere: but it's never been difficult to arrange for some justice to be done. In fact, once the story got out about what had happened, I was fielding calls from all over the city, offering to give Charlie what he deserved.

Chivalry is not dead and neither is organized crime in Chicago, for that matter. The Blue Island crew thought it would be best to find him while he was out, pick a fight with him and make sure he wasn't able to walk away from it. The boys from Bridgeport offered to bust his knees out, quickly and quietly while I was in Memphis for another emotional recovery period. While each idea was tempting, I opted to handle things more maturely. There are enough nutcases in the world.

Take my aunt, for example. She's always been the loon of the family for as long as I can remember, and for the most part, she was deemed harmless. But one evening after my uncle broke plans with her, she followed him into the bathroom with a twelve gauge shotgun. The story is that he laughed it off and told her she didn't know how to use it. Without hesitation, she cocked the rifle and aimed at his face. He was in the tub and was able to duck underwater when she fired the first round. The gun blew a huge hole in the wall and needless to say their plans for the evening were back on track. Then what? They lived happily ever after? You bet. And that is just insane to me.

Kit Campbell

I've never been in a relationship where fighting was involved and I've always been proud of not taking any action post-break. When it's done, it's done. But let me tell you something: when you are deceived so greatly, crazy is going to be calling. Willing or not, I entertained the notion of answering that call.

I started drifting off into sick fantasies of getting myself back into the house, handcuffing him to the radiator, then tossing his cell phone in the toilet and telling him that no one was coming to help him. I had lectures lined up in my head while he sat on the floor and was forced to listen. Maybe I'd tape his mouth shut, but then maybe I'd like to hear him cry and say to himself, "This is not happening".

I'd be perfect in every sequence. I wouldn't be disheveled or irate. I'd be passionate, articulate and convincingly pissed off. The scenes in my mind were getting more drastic by the day and ultimately each one was a little crazy.

Realistically, I would never be able to pull off something of that sort. The problem with confrontation is just that. I'd have to put myself in that situation and maintain all control. With deranged thoughts like that bouncing around in my head, losing control wasn't something I wanted to volunteer for.

Then there's the idea of tampering with his assets. It's pretty simple. If your car doesn't run, you can't make it to work. If you can't make it to work, you can't pay your rent. Now who's got the rain cloud over their head?

Thank goodness he was dumb enough to give me the passwords to his email accounts, which presented me with the option of causing some trouble that way. From employment resignations to date cancellations, it was all at my fingertips. Have I gone stark raving mad?

It's true that I developed a one track mind that revolved around revenge. He did bad things to good people and he had to be stopped. Would I tell his new girlfriend of his shady doings, complete with photographic evidence? Would I warn the others not to trust him as I presented the facts? What was I going to do?

Spilled Milk

I had not yet made a move in any direction. Crazy kept calling me up and had me believing that it was okay to be thinking these demented thoughts. There was a bottom line here somewhere, and I needed to find it. Was it that I just wasn't like him? I just wasn't one of those people who hurt others, whether they deserve it or not.

But then, maybe it was that because no matter how much I hated him at that moment, I loved him more. In theory, horrible things happening to someone who hurt you sounds pretty good. But in reality, when that same person happens to be someone you adored, it just doesn't sound so good anymore.

Although my hysterical fantasies would have been rather therapeutic to live out, it would have been crazy nonetheless. Besides who needs a kidnapping and criminal property damage conviction on their record? Not me. Messing with his assets is just psychotic. Besides, messing with his car and home would be entirely too "south side" of me, and I couldn't allow him to relish that stereotype.

Altering his calendar and causing disaster via the internet would have been easy and completely flawless, however totally insane. Furthermore, he was slowly plotting his own personal demise and probably didn't need any help. What goes around may come around, but crazy stays with you. There are lines everywhere and sometimes when you cross, it's not easy to go back.

If anything, I wished he would remember me as the girl he never should have left behind. I'd love it if he occasionally wondered where I was and whom I was with. I'd never want to go down in the books as that psycho he made the mistake of giving a ring to. It was bad enough that it was over, but it was important for me to remain the good guy.

It's not like I came to this conclusion easily. I was still angry as hell and hurting from all those knives in my back. But the pain was starting to fade and every day that went by, I felt less and less like I needed to go out with a bang.

I had the absolute power over many different aspects of his well being. I suppose it just wasn't in my nature to abuse such a power. But there was strength in knowing that the ability to alter his circumstances

Kit Campbell

was *all mine*. It was like holding something over his head without him even knowing it. I had the finally found the truth. Perhaps taking action was unnecessary.

The way I see it, you have all the right in the world to feel how you feel. What the two of you are experiencing is not the same. The only thing he feels is sorry. But in exchange, you feel cold, nasty, unrelenting pain. Whether it's warranted or not, that's the way it is. Who do you think it's worse for? So be disgusted. Be angry. When the smoke clears, even years down the line, bet that he is still that sorry son of a bitch that you remember. So be enraged. Be sickened. Just don't be crazy.

BURY THE HATCHET

A few years ago, my two sister in laws talked me into taking a Pilates class with them. It was supposed to be one of those bonding things that the three of us could do together, and it would have been productive, as opposed to meeting up for dinner and drinks. So, reluctantly, I went along with it. We were doomed from the start. Not only was one of my old high school teachers one of my new classmates, but our room was surrounded by windows. Anyone walking the halls of the park district had the pleasure of seeing us, not only in horrible clothing, but in extremely unflattering positions.

We were the chronic gigglers in the class. Whether our coach was talking her neo tree hugging cosmic language or if we couldn't compose ourselves after a classmate's accidental flatulence, we seemed to be laughing all the time. You'd have thought that we'd start taking things a little more seriously after the instructor separated us, but no such luck. It was just too funny.

Something we found particularly amusing, were the meditation exercises we had to do before the end of each class. She would coach us through breathing techniques and help us visualize a scenario that she'd walk us through. Each time we were supposed to be one step closer to inner peace.

I remember our instructor asking us to close our eyes and picture our worst enemy. She asked us to look this person in the eye and remember what brought us to this point. After silently rehashing the situation, whatever it may have been, you visualize giving said person a forgiving embrace. This was supposed to cleanse your mind of negative thoughts and memories. It was a way to bury an emotional hatchet; or some nonsense.

Our teacher gave detailed directions while guiding the class and everyone seemed to be really be moved by it. Everyone except for us,

61

that is. We were too busy making faces and trying to make each other laugh during the silence.

On the way home, the girls and I were discussing how pointless the exercise was for us, because we didn't really have any enemies. Sure, there was that one bimbo back in high school that I always imagined myself smacking the hell out of, but one of my friends had beaten me to the punch. Besides, I wouldn't have considered her an enemy. She was just the average blonde that you love to hate. Doesn't every high school have one of those?

Then I got to thinking. Who would I seriously consider to be my enemy? Was it that girl who looked like a frog that happened to lose her virginity to my boyfriend at the time? No, she was just an idiot and they're everywhere.

It's almost as if you have to be threatened by someone in order to place them at enemy status. A true enemy would probably be someone you trusted in the past, but were betrayed by. This is someone who let you down like you never imagined. But I honestly couldn't think of anyone who filled that void. What a comforting thought.

Now fast forward to the days following the Charlie trauma. In fact, let's skip right to those sleepless nights. Countless thoughts filled my brain while I was lying in bed peeking at the clock and crying. My poor head was pounding in torment and I was begging God to make it stop. He must not have been listening because my only relief was secret stash of very potent sleeping pills and I knew I couldn't keep that up forever. Not only was it extraordinarily expensive, but my sleep deprivation was starting to show on the outside. I needed help.

It was there in the dark that I made a discovery. There was in fact, someone who hurt me so bad that I was still in disbelief. He was the same person I had been crying over, the one who left me on my knees.

Isn't it strange how the ones we care for so immensely, are the often the ones who are capable of hurting us like no other? I had held him up so high for so long, but the truth remained. This man who spoke of how he loved me for the longest time ended up taking the first train out of town and never looked back. He may as well have driven me out to the middle

Spilled Milk

of a desert and left me there. Admittedly, it was probably something he didn't enjoy doing, but nonetheless, he did it. His indifference alone was enough to transform my love into the closest thing I ever had to an enemy. Anyone who could do something that awful to me was worthy of that title; no matter how much it hurt me to admit.

So I closed my eyes and pictured him. Just looking at him made it hurt right away. I opened my eyes to darkness and that dreaded clock advancing into the morning. I had to shake it off. I had to find a way to rest my head. My lack of sleep was becoming apparent to everyone around me. If anyone needed some peace of mind, it was me.

Again, I shut my eyes and pictured myself in front of him. We were looking into each other's eyes and could feel the storm surrounding us. I felt the hate I had for him leaving me the way he did and the love I had since I first saw him. I looked up at him, and into his dark eyes, then took his strong hands and wrapped his arms around me. He held me tight just like he used to and I could barely breathe. Fight to inhale: I felt his breath but had none of my own. Tighter now than ever before, but I started to let go. We began to separate but froze with our faces just inches apart. His eyes were sorry and mine moved to the floor. I let him go and he was gone. Exhale.

That was the last thing I remember before I fell asleep that night. But that was the beauty of it all. I had a chance to rest my head and have some peace, if only for a few hours. What a relief to finally drift into the bliss of sleep. There have been plenty of time since then that I have broken down in tears over him, but never again did it disturb my precious sleep.

Who would have thought that something I believed was so silly years ago, would bring me such contentment in an unexpected time of need? I had a chance to bury the hatchet. But you know me, I didn't dig too deep.

63

LITTLE MISS REBOUND

Now what was I supposed to do? How was I going to play it this time around? Would I kick off my shoes and go back to better living through chemistry? Or would I lace them up tight and tell the coach to put me back in the game? Get ready to sound the buzzer; there's about to be a rebound.

I had seen him around. He's a well known musician in Chicago and we knew plenty of the same people, but never each other. I felt an introduction was necessary, so I stepped up and threw him a line. He went for it; hook, line and sinker. That was Chad.

Coincidentally, he had just ended a relationship around the same time mine ended, we so were in the same boat. We didn't want anything more than fun. And let me just say, we had some fun! So much, in fact, that I wasn't sure I'd hear from him after that first crazy night. But I did because apparently, he'd had just as good a time. I knew from day one that he wasn't boyfriend material whatsoever, but I also knew that I really liked him anyway.

Luckily his gigs were predominately held on weekends, so I'd found someone to spend my newfound time with. Being with Chad was like a breath of fresh air. He was intelligent, funny and talented beyond belief. Not to mention, looks damn good in a wife beater. But I think what really got me was that he was completely carefree. His energy and perspective were contagious and we were headed for good times. If ever I was Bonnie, he would have been my Clyde.

Having Chad around was a complete lifestyle change for me. There was no need to get up for work, so why not stay out all night, every night? I was having fun. How else can you explain brushing up on our lindy hop in a parking lot at 6am? Or talking my dad into an extremely late night poker game? Or just falling asleep together in front of the

Spilled Milk

TV, two hours after the sun had come up. Nothing major, but we were having fun.

He didn't quite reach all the requirements on my hefty list of standards, but it didn't matter. He wasn't even interested in trying. He was just in it for the ride. So I gave him one. Besides, it's just a rebound, right?

I was the same to him. In fact, we were friendly enough to joke about it; that's just how well we were able to communicate. It was all jokes and fun, Chad's two favorite things, besides music and women.

And there were women. Who wouldn't be attracted to a good looking musician with a smile that could talk you into anything?

I didn't want to say it, but I had to. If he was going to hit the sheets with me, he couldn't with anyone else. I told him that if he met a girl that he liked more than me, to go for it. All I asked is that he pondered that for a moment before making any decisions, because once you leave, you can't come back. This was more for safety's sake than to present boundaries. And without hesitation, he agreed. We were to be exclusive, but not serious.

I worried about it hitting a serious level the first time he told me that he loved me. But after it happened a few times, I realized that it was only his liquid courage coming through and it probably meant nothing.

"Give yourself some time," I told him, "you'll change your mind".

Damn, I'm good. Spring flew by and by summertime, we were lucky to get together once a week. Maybe it was that he had more gigs than before, but maybe it was a lack of interest. What once was hot and heavy had simmered down to nightly phone calls. The thrill had dissipated and we were left to our conversation. Who knew we would have actually liked each other?

I worried we'd crossed the friendship line when there were no more kisses hello and goodbye, but the calls kept coming in. And it got to the point when I would be surprised when he put his hands on me. Our basic encounters had changed drastically, but as long as he kept dialing me up, I went along with it.

Kit Campbell

We both swore from the beginning that we wouldn't get too attached, but ended up doing it anyway. The problem with rebounds is that they can easily be transformed into a safety net. Neither of us was scoring big anymore. We just wanted what everyone else wants: someone to catch you, in case you fall.

REPEAT OFFENDERS

I've always been a chronic door locker. Perhaps it's a slight case of OCD, but my dad has always been the same way. We maintain that it is simply for safety's sake. If someone belongs beyond the lock, they'll already have a key. If not, they have to ask for permission to come in. I'm all for that.

A good thing to keep in mind is that just because someone leaves, doesn't mean they won't come back. They always do, don't they? You know, sooner or later? It usually happens, like most things, when you least suspect. As soon as you have completed erasing them from your mind, they pop up out of nowhere and turn your world upside down all over again.

It was August and I was just kicking off my usual week long birthday celebration. My brother, Frank and I were downtown seeing our favorite band. After following them for years, we finally met the guys, shared a bottle of Jack Daniels with our heroes on the bus and were right in front of the sound board for the show. I was having what I considered thus far, the best time of my life.

Who knows what made me stop dancing and take the time to check my phone, but I did and I couldn't believe my eyes. I stopped moving all together and whether or not it was the substance abuse of the night, I thought I was going to fall down. I handed the phone to Frank because I wanted to see if I was imagining this. It couldn't be, but it was....a message from Perry.

Damn near two years had gone by and not a peep from him. And now, in the middle of such bliss, appeared a huge downer. Why now? I thought I was going to cry and I wanted to leave the booth and hide. But Frank wouldn't allow it. He took my phone and put it in his pocket. "Not now," he said, then lit a smoke and got me dancing again.

Kit Campbell

The show was incredible, as it always is and the positivity surrounding us helped me fight whatever it was that I was feeling. Shock, confusion, sadness: be gone! I couldn't let it touch me because on a night like that, Frank and I were truly untouchable. Mentally and physically, we were high as kites and thank God I have him to protect me from being brought down.

We went back to the tour bus and hung out after the show. More faded than my favorite jeans, we spent hours with our idols, laughing and talking and have a great time. Eventually, we made our way back to the south side but we were so excited about the events of the evening, that the subject of Perry was miles away. That is, until we got back home, of course.

Our folks were still awake and we didn't even try to hide that we were completely under the influence. We were just too excited for anything like that. We gushed to them about our night and how much fun we'd had together. Frank thanked me profusely for giving him the chance to have such an experience and I told him that I couldn't imagine doing it without him. As long as we were storytelling, I had to tell my mom about the message I'd received earlier in the night.

Should I call him back? Of course I wanted to, but I was afraid to bring my dreamlike night to a crashing halt. Mom advised that because I was on top of the world now, that I should call him immediately, even though it was the wee hours of the morning. She thought my happiness would bleed through the phone line and it would make him that much happier to hear from me. Besides, he'd left the message early in the night and I'd made him wait long enough. So with a glass of water to help sober me up, I headed to my room to make the call.

He was still awake and as big of a smartass as I'd remembered. I loved that about him. There was no awkward silence; just the two of us, yammering back and forth playing the catch up game. He became an uncle, traveled often and when I heard him laugh, I remembered how much I loved him.

So much had happened since we had last spoken and even with his updates, I couldn't find out why he had called in the first place. Still, we talked until after the sun came up. He did mention that I was on

Spilled Milk

his mind at one point in our conversation, along with plenty of our moments together; which in some cases, I was impressed by his memory. But still, why now? Why after all this time? I didn't dare ask and when I couldn't keep my eyes open any longer, I decided to say goodnight.

"So now what?" he asked me. "I guess I'll just call you in a year or so?"

From one smartass to another, "Sounds good. Talk to you in a year or so".

We hung up and I was right back in love with him. It happened that fast again. I got under the covers and smiled as I replayed our conversation in my head. Then, I got the best sleep I'd had since the last time he was sleeping next to me.

In fact, I slept right through the first two text messages he sent me that afternoon. He was going to be in my area later that day and all that talk about our favorite restaurant had put a thought into this head. He'll call me later.

You better believe I was looking my best by dinnertime. This was my shot to make it happen; all the things we used to talk about doing were no longer impossible anymore. I knew he could come back.

Or would he? After waiting for two hours, like a jilted prom date, I received a text message explaining that he'd been caught up and would make it up to me sometime soon. I felt like a failure and wanted to crawl into bed. But I didn't. I've gotten over you once, I don't need to do it again. Besides as long as I was looking good, someone was going to see me.

A few weeks went by and it was Perry's birthday. I had not heard from him but sent him a hilarious private joke via text with my birthday greetings. Back and forth, that went on for a few days. And then, silence.

By this time, I'd found my latest distractions. I was invited to LA for the final show of a friend's North American tour. Two days after my return, I started a new gig. I was full time at a station over 75 miles from

Kit Campbell

home, so I moved from the south side to the north side to be closer. Yeah, I kept myself busy.

After settling into my new place, all I could think of was inviting him over. This was my first place all by myself, in the city, and I wanted him to see it. I was proud. This was something we wanted to do and I was doing it, with or without him.

He seemed genuinely excited when I told him and said how proud of me he was. Plus, he offered to help me work on my parallel parking, due to my awful driving record. He even went so far as to tease me about buying a queen when I know how much he likes California kings. He couldn't wait to see it! How's Friday?

Don't be surprised by the silence. That's just the sound of Perry never calling for directions. We'll never know why he stopped calling or even why he started up again in the first place.

By midnight that Friday night, I was in bed with some pharmaceutical help and I was holding my phone. Thank goodness for that, or I would have missed a late night call from Chad, who was performing in the area. Although I never told him, he seemed to know what I was going through, because he snapped back from 'friend Chad' to 'can't keep his hands off of me Chad'. It was perfect timing because if I needed anything that night, it was affection. Safety nets save lives.

I loved Chad for that, but it wasn't the same kind of love that I had for Perry. Why did I still see a future with someone who wouldn't give me the time of day?

I had totally jumped the gun, not that he was fully aware. We weren't getting back together and our relationship was ancient history, so what was I thinking? I suppose just because someone comes back, doesn't mean they're going to stay. That was a tough lesson to learn.

But I had learned the hardest lesson long ago; how to carry on every day without him. I already knew how to do that. I wasn't going to allow myself a recovery period this time. Today would be like any other day; without him.

Spilled Milk

And that was it. I closed the door on Perry. I felt a light inside of me dim, but I think that deep down there will always be a flicker of hope. That's the beauty of it, really. You can close the door, but you don't have to lock it.

WHAT IT IS

Deciding whether you'll sink or swim should be an instant decision, but I managed to contemplate it for quite some time. With the possibility of Perry's return having been crushed and the Charlie debacle long behind me, where it belongs, I didn't have much to look forward to, in that department. That is, except for my nightly phone calls with Chad.

He had somehow become the one person I talked to about everything. Well, everything except for our status. Still, I was lucky enough to have him involved, via the phone lines, to my new everyday life.

He was the one would go to great lengths to entertain me on a nightly basis. Whether he would follow up on my daily happenings or call to share a song he'd written, he was the one who was most involved in my world, though from a distance.

Maintaining our relationship was no easy task, though it seemed to be, for him. I often wondered how I could be so emotionally close to someone who was seemingly undisturbed by our geographical distance. It was as though I was subjecting myself to an otherwise involuntary bout of emotional S&M. I wanted him near me so badly and sometimes wondered if that was the reason he stayed away.

We'd connected from day one, and while the romance had died out, we both needed to stay in contact with one another. We'd both become dependent on the thought that the other would always be there. But soon, for me, that was no longer enough. Apparently, I needed more to hold than my cell phone.

The time had come to separate what was there between us and what was not. We had laughter, a reliable friendship and obvious likeability, but no love. With such a driving force remaining absent, there was no wonder why we just weren't going anywhere anymore. Just off to bed! We'll talk, hang up and go to bed.

Spilled Milk

At the time it seemed like a good idea to be honest with him. I always was. I could no longer keep him as a priority when he kept me as an option. It just wasn't fair to me and when it started to hurt bad enough, I let him in on my thoughts. Let's try it, like normal people do. You know, give it a shot.

What a laugh that was! If I didn't have such a good sense of humor, I might have cried through the entire discussion. Chad managed to turn each of my questions into answers surrounded by riddles. Nothing but jokes and fun for him; I should have seen this coming.

Apparently Chad saw my proposition for wanting more, as wanting way too much. He wasn't ready for anything like that and was pleased with our current standing. But I wasn't content with being left in the middle ground. I'm an all or nothing kind of girl and wasn't sure if I could take it any longer.

I couldn't make any sense of his telling me that he's not ready for a serious relationship yet he's attracted to me and sees me in his life until it's over. How does one translate something like that? He thinks I only hear certain parts of our conversation, and he's right. Those are the things I remember you telling me. Those were as close to the answers as I was going to get. Of course that's what I held onto as we talked. Finally, he provided the concrete answer I'd feared

"If you're looking for white picket fences, you're looking in the wrong place."

While completely necessary to hear, those words were the equivalent to a punch in the stomach. But once I was able to catch my breath, I realized that I had to take my friendship with Chad for exactly what it was, friendship and nothing more.

Honesty, though sometimes brutal, can certainly shed some light on a subject. I've never had to actually accept a bargain like that before. Was this something I could handle? Could I bury my feelings for him and enjoy a straight out friendship with Chad? Or would I trash the whole thing because it didn't work out as planned?

Kit Campbell

In Chad, I found so many amazing qualities and sometimes I wish other people could just see what I see in him. Being without him would be a lot like missing out on something for me. How could I turn him away? Both of us suffer that way and why?

Chad expressed several times that he wanted me in his life, for as long as he was alive. I couldn't see it any other way. Someone actually saw themselves next to me throughout moments of the rest of his life: and told me. No, it wasn't romantic, but it was sincere. It wasn't loving, but it was genuine. I like the idea of knowing him until the end of my days and reached a compromise in that thought. Just because I couldn't have him like that, didn't mean I could have him, at all.

He had the ability to not only knock the wind out of me, but breathe new life into me on the same night, there was no way I was going to say goodbye. I gained an incredible person on my cast roster and plan to keep him there. He may not always be so apparent and our place on each other's totem pole is bound to eventually drop. I realize that. But we've been blessed to find in each other what others sometimes just can't see. Only a fool would turn down something as remarkable as that.

So maybe it was never a question as to choose to sink or swim. In this capacity, we just wanted to be alongside one another for the ride. So we continue down the winding roads of our lives and keep it on cruise control.

GO TEAM GO

When did women stop backing each other and launch this treacherous cold war between one another? Does this go back to the beginning of time?

I know firsthand how natural it comes to just dislike other women, mainly when they've taken over my role. And it's not only me; I really think it comes as an instinct for all of us.

So, I'm surfing the web with my friend and stumble upon an online profile Perry had created, along with pictures posted of him and the girl that came right after me. Immediately, my friend and I tore her to shreds.

"Holy horseface, Batman!"

"And what's with that crunchy, 1980s perm?"

We really had a field day at this girl's expense. No, she couldn't hear us, but the words were said, nonetheless. I almost started feeling guilty about how ruthless our insults were becoming. But truth be told, I despised everything about her.

I hated her giant forehead and her nappy hair. I hated that she was a Cubs fan and I hated her big, toothy smile. But most of all, I hated her arms around the man that used to really love me.

And then reality set in: maybe he really loved her, too. Maybe she told great jokes and was a good cook. Maybe she was sincere and awfully friendly. Who knows? Maybe she wasn't all that bad. If he loved her, she couldn't be.

This is just a prime example of the angel and the devil that sit on my shoulders, constantly arguing with each other. The red guy wants me to hate her and curse her name for eternity. The white one suggests a more

Kit Campbell

peaceful approach and pushes toward understanding. Here I am stuck in the middle.

"Stop arguing you two, and let me think!"

I think I could dislike her if she were a liar or a crabass. I'd hate if she were tasteless and vulgar and I'd certainly be disgusted if she were crass or trashy. The fact is I had no idea if she was any of these things. The only thing I had to go on, was a picture of her next to him. Again, my yin and yang are fighting.

White One, "You know, I hate to admit it, but she kind of does have a pretty smile."

Red Guy, "What are you....blind?"

Honestly, the premise of an uncalled for "me vs. you" mindset is not only absurd but unacceptable. Horseface or not, keep in mind the formula that men require: Outer beauty catches them, inner beauty keeps them. Don't compare yourself to others because each one of us is so different.

We need to start supporting and celebrating each other as women again. There is nothing wrong with enjoying each other. Do not make enemies based on the pursuit of men. Sure, there is a natural competition born between us, but better to build an army, than to try to take one on.

I decided to try this theory just recently and was pleasantly surprised with the results. I was at a west coast swing show with a friend of mine, when he drew attention to a few ladies that were whispering and pointing in my direction.

To my horror, there she was: the girl that Chad was dating. We'd never met in person, but clearly knew of each other. As she whispered to her friends and pointed at me, I knew I was up against them, with or without reason. Now I could have cackled with my date and made mention of her gopher-like facial expressions, but instead, I grabbed my clutch and walked right up to the bar next to them.

76

Spilled Milk

I ordered a grey goose martini and waited for my drink as they looked on. My friend was watching me work from across the room and their sudden silence really put the pressure on. I had to do something.

"I love those shoes," I told her. "How you can dance so well in them is beyond me!"

BAM!! That's when the winds changed. They were flabbergasted, but my strategic move had actually worked. The next thing you know, these girls are buying me drinks and asking where I got my dress. It wasn't as awful as it could have been, for anyone. And my theory was proven positive.

Slander and cattiness are so unattractive. I'm not asking anyone to ignore their instinctual competitive nature. But there is certainly such a thing as friendly competition. I think that's a fair compromise, don't you? Are you with me on this, ladies? Now get out there and show 'em what you got. Let the games begin!

THE KEYMASTER

I think the Ghostbusters were really onto something with that whole keymaster/gatekeeper thing. One, without the other, just doesn't work. So what do you do? Get those two together and see what happens. It could be the end of the world, but then again, you never know.

So I've got the key, I'm convinced. I've got the key to the future and how I envision it to be. All I needed was to find the one who would let me unlock them and take them with me. For the longest time, I really believed it was him and to some extent, I still wanted to believe it. I owed myself the minimum of curing my curiosity: must see Perry.

What better day than New Years Eve in Chicago? Not only did I secretly recall this day in years prior to when he asked me to be his girl, but more appropriately, the Bears were playing the Packers at Soldier Field. Dad handed Frank and I tickets at the last minute and wouldn't you just know it? Perry is a season ticket holder.

This gave me a great excuse to contact him and while we didn't meet up at the game, we'd made arrangements for him to come by two days later. While I was weary from being stood up the last time we'd made plans, he surprised me pleasantly by showing up and on time.

I was expecting the button-down guy I used to love like no other, but was greeted by a bearded beatnik. Nonetheless, he was just as beautiful as I remembered. My chatterbox button was pushed because there's something about hearing him laugh that makes me happy. He stayed late into the evening with me and ended up leaving with not as much as a casual hug goodbye. But because the physical contact petrified me as well, I brushed it off and told him, "Yes, I'd like to see you again".

We did not make plans again for a few more weeks, which gave me plenty of time to think about our encounter. Apparently I am a master in the ways of over analyzing. While I was pleased to see him, he left me

Spilled Milk

with a strong feeling of discontent that I just couldn't shake. Why was I feeling this way?

Was it the little things that were bothering me? For example, could it have been that my apartment had its first squeaky-cleaning due to his arrival and his only remark about my new place was that it reminded him of a doctor's office? Forget the thirty pounds I'd lost, could it have been that I looked smashing after working a ten hour day and with two years of not seeing me, not so much as a generic compliment? I just couldn't wrap my head around the idea that I was still asking for too much. Hell, I didn't expect him to wear a shirt that said "I love Kit" or anything, but it wouldn't have killed him to show a little warmth.

After thinking over what I had thought over, I decided I was being much too selfish. We really didn't know each other anymore and that became the task at hand.

I'll say that during our telephone conversations there was definitely sporadic laughter, but I'd nearly forgotten the kind of rapport we once had with one another. We were very sarcastic, nitpicky and constantly in 'keep each other in check' mode. I always remembered him sending me away floating, but this time around, I was feeling exhausted, more than anything.

There was a newfound lack of effort on his behalf and it was noticeable and rather jarring. From extended delays in message response and shallowly recognizing his apathy toward his appearance, to last minute date cancellations; he was screaming "I don't care!".

Seeing as his idols include the likes of Peter Griffin and Al Bundy, I shouldn't have been surprised by his behavior, but I sure was. Perhaps it would have gone unnoticed if we knew each other differently, but unlike Peg, I just don't see myself dolling up to get attention from someone who'd be just as happy falling asleep on my couch. That's the average man and I always held him up so much higher.

I'll admit that sounds like I'm on a high horse, so I'll step it down a notch. Peg and Al Bundy are married and Lord knows I will probably have plenty to say by the time I'm married for twenty years. But now, so soon into whatever it was we were getting into? I found the lack of effort

Kit Campbell

to be quite unacceptable and began drifting away in my front to show lack of interest.

Perry is all I ever thought I wanted. Had I painted our history through memory in a lovelier shade than the truth? Or had we both changed so much that it terrified me into thinking, maybe this isn't what I want.

That isn't what happened in Ghostbusters! The keymaster and the gatekeeper didn't meet for coffee and separate before trying to accomplish something! But then again, this isn't Ghostbusters, come to think of it. Nonetheless, I'm convinced I've got the key to unlocking some pretty amazing things. Could it be that all this time I was waiting outside the wrong gate? I'd better put this key in a safe place and think about that.

IN THE DARK

Is it always darkest before the dawn? Is there even the smallest possibility that one can't notice the darkness because they have surrounded themselves in light? And even more disturbing, what about the ones who can't ever see light because they're used to it being so dark?

It's a dangerous street to walk on and I know it like the back of my hand. That reason alone is probably how I recognized what Perry was going through. But shame on me, I ignored it and hoped it wasn't real.

The first time I raised an eyebrow, we were out in the suburbs for a catch up session, over long island iced teas. When I could no longer tiptoe around my need to discover why he'd started coming back around, he told me. It wasn't romantic or even the acceptable cover of pure curiosity. It was sad and probably very true:

"I've made nothing but bad decisions since you".

When he elaborated, it was apparent that after we separated he'd bought a one way ticket down the tubes, or at least that's how he felt about his decisions. I wanted to shake it off and consider it to be the closest thing to romantic he'd been since reuniting with me, so I did.

Then there was the first time since our break that he was going to see my brother, Frank. A group of us got tickets for a movie at the IMAX at Navy Pier, so we made a day out of it. It was an early afternoon show and after parking the cars, Perry was on a mission to find the bar. Mind you, this is a guy who drinks mainly at sporting events and doesn't hold liquor very well, which is why he opted to be a doper. I know this. I loved that about him. But now, I'm chasing after him down the maze around the pier wanting to know why he needed a drink so badly. The group split for about a half hour, due to long bathroom lines, last minute ATM visits and apparently, a vodka break. I didn't notice until we took our seats in the theatre and I smelled it on him. That time, I didn't raise an eyebrow. It was more of a shaking my head kind of thing.

Kit Campbell

Later, a gathering at my house found everyone at the table, playing cards and Perry alone, in the front room with no lights on. My guests kept giving me awkward eyes and I didn't know how to react. I kept asking him to join us and he would, for five minutes at a time and then go back to the dark. He kept asking me to stay in the room with him, but I had to put my foot down.

"I'm not going to stay here in the dark with you. We have company. Now get out here."

At soon as the words came out of my mouth, it hit me. I said, "we", when there was no such thing as "we" anymore. Terms like "we" and "us" and our" no longer applied and it was an anchor that I just couldn't agree to carry around anymore.

I thought to myself, "*We* don't have problems, *you* do".

I realize how harsh that sounds in retrospect. But it was coming from my gut, so I had no choice but to acknowledge the truth. Here's where it became even more difficult for me. I remember telling Perry when we were breaking up that it would always be alright for him to come back. I said if he ever needed me that he should let me know. I remembered promising him that I would love him no matter what.

Now, I know I meant those things when I said them, but clearly was not thinking about the long term repercussions that may have popped up down the line. I suppose when someone's telling you they have a hard time getting out of bed and facing the day, that it's important to solidify your stance. So I did.

When my guests left, we were finally alone. He's been sick with sadness for so long and it was written all over him. He told me he was aware that he wasn't hiding it very well anymore and I just wanted to hold him. I wanted to play with his hair until he fell asleep and just hold onto him like I used to when he was having a tough time. But I didn't. I thought my words would be more effective this time around.

So I told him again and I meant it again. If you need a hand up, I've got two. I always want to hear from you, it's always ok to call. I want to see you and even more, I want to see you smile. I want you to be happy;

82

Spilled Milk

if you need anything just tell me. I can't read your mind, so you've got to tell me. I'm telling you right now, no matter what happens, I will always care about you.

There was no passionate kiss to follow. This was so much bigger than that. It did not revolve around what I wanted anymore. It was my purpose to be the brightest star outside his dark planet; a flashlight in the cave, so to speak. Without words I had begged to be, and was given that position.

Before he left he said something to me that he'd said a few times since we'd gotten back in contact.

"I need you to have faith ".

Then I said something to him that I have always wanted to say, "I do,". And I meant it.

Slowly he started to participate in his own life again. There were outings and vacations I heard about, but was not a part of. Oddly enough, I started to hear happiness in his voice again, which was enough to satisfy me.

Learning to become selfless in our recent days was certainly taxing on me. But there was a notion that I just couldn't ignore: I must have been something special. Knowing that was enough to get by.

In his darkest hour, who did he turn to? I cannot accept credit for his turn for the better, but I'm certainly proud and flattered that he would have come to me, even if all he wanted was to hear that everything would be alright. I must have really meant something to him for Perry to think he still meant anything to me. Truth be told, he always will.

Anyone who has ever lived in the dark and been unexplainably saddened knows that it's a lonely and frightening place to be. Those who have come into the light will tell you, all you really need is a flashlight and someone who truly cares, to tell you that everything is going to be ok.

MAKE THAT MOVE

Another Hallmark holiday was upon us and I crawled out from under my hangover to greet this year's Sweetest Day. It was almost 3pm when I popped a few Excedrin and heard my cell phone ringing.

Did you know that Sweetest Day is only a Midwestern holiday? It's true. Ask my family in Jersey about Sweetest Day and they'll tell you you've got a screw loose! I can't imagine Perry was even aware that he was Sweetest Day when he called and asked me to have lunch with him, but I hoped he did anyway. That's the hopeless romantic in me; keyword being 'hopeless'.

Apparently he had something very important to tell me and I felt a panic slip over me as I did my best to pull myself together after a rather late night. He didn't give me much time. He was calling from right outside my house.

Just what did he have to tell me? What was so important that he wants to tell me, in person, right now? Did he meet someone? Or even worse, did he get her pregnant? Oh God. What is it?

I slid into his car and he drove us to a pizzeria in the next neighborhood. Whether it was a belly full of last night's alcohol or my nerves, I could hardly eat. I was trying so hard to play it cool, but I was dying to hear the news.

"So?"

"So I'm moving out this way".

Hallelujah! There was no pregnant girlfriend. I breathed a silent sigh of relief. And I was shocked. After paying the mortgage for the house he grew up in for almost ten years, I worried he'd never escape and start a life of his own. He'd been guilted into submission for so long that this move to the city seemed rather sudden. But most of all, I was happy.

Spilled Milk

This was a big step in the right direction for Perry, not to mention it would bring him closer to me.

I understand he was fielding a lot of guilt from his friends and family for leaving the suburbs, so he was pleased to hear that I was proud of him for making that move. Come the end of the month, Perry would be a city boy again!

A few weeks later, he stopped by to pick up some things I'd gathered for his new place. It seemed he wasn't getting much help from anyone, so I took donations of small appliances and unused household items to help get him settled. He promised once he got his new Wrigleyville apartment in order, that he'd have me over for a housewarming.

I needed to be sure that were weren't becoming Jerry and Elaine here. I was not at all interested in a casual friendship with him, just because we'd be neighbors. I couldn't love, love, love him if he would never love me back. It seemed I had a move to make as well.

My friend, Lily, who has extensive experience with successfully reviving relationships always gave great advice and helped me lay out a game plan. I was to ease my way into his new home, so that he was comfortable with having me there, more often than not and preferably more so than the possible visiting friends and family.

I'd always imagined putting together a home with him and I couldn't wait to get started. Sure, I was thought it would be our home, but this was the closest thing reality had to offer and I was prepared to participate.

It panicked me to think of how I'd put the moves on him after all this time. Would he deny me? Would he give in to the weakness of the flesh, if only for one night? Or would we touch, hear trumpets, and live happily ever after?

I feel like that owl in the old Tootsie Pop commercials I grew up watching, because really, "The world may never know".

Months went by and I never heard from him. I worried he fell back into his depression. I wondered if he'd found someone who could finally

85

make him smile the way I'd been trying to for so long. I suppose I could pick up the phone and get some answers, right?

Wrong. My patience had worn thin. It was no longer my responsibility to check up on him. How many times was I supposed to offer help, only to be treated like a crutch that's kept in the closet? I had my fill of being acknowledged as a liability rather than an asset. It no longer was a question of my love for him, which for some reason just won't fade; but instead a barometer for my own self respect. It was yet another round of Perry making the conscious decision that his life would be better without me in it. It was done.

We coexist only a few miles from one another and behave as though nothing ever happened at all. How ironic that after the excitement of relocation, the only way I could ever truly move forward was not to make a move at all.

PRESERVATIVES ADDED

Why do preservatives have such a bad name? We've grown anxious over the idea of their hazards but has anyone stopped to think of their benefits? Sure, food and the rest of life have their differences, but do you see where I'm going with this?

Making a decision and having the conviction to see it through are two different stories entirely. I had made up my mind in regards to Perry but searched for further reasoning to solidify my stance. This requisition for solidarity wasn't so much for the day to day, but rather for the long haul. I needed to remind myself of the real reasons why I shouldn't pick up the phone and revive this ever again.

I always knew he'd come back, but never thought it would have been anything like this. Why was I so worried and uncomfortable with everything involving Perry? This was so unlike me. I was self conscious, uncertain and afraid. I was suffocating in skepticism. I couldn't recognize myself anymore.

This was a self preservation emergency. I needed to take a long hard look in the mirror and decipher exactly who that girl is, staring back at me: what she is and what she is not. I needed to remove the wrong and preserve the right.

A friend of mine taught me something a few years ago, about keeping your emotions in check so that no matter how strong they are, they can never defeat you. She suggested a feeding session in front of the mirror. Sure, take five minutes and be sad. Watch yourself cry and know the reason is someone else, because you can control that girl in the glass. If you want her stop crying, just make her stop crying. The same would go with feeling guilty. Sit down and watch yourself be the villain. After five minutes, knock it off and carry on with the rest of your life. The same would be fitting for all kinds of feelings like pride, happiness or even if you're just feeling sorry for yourself. I was determined to find

Kit Campbell

some peace on the subject and was willing to try anything. Hell, no one's looking…

So I sat down and had a staring contest with the girl in the mirror. She was apprehensive at first, which surprised me. This isn't like her, to be so spiritless, so careful. Who is this girl?

Staring into your own eyes can be so incredible. The thoughts that run through your mind range from exhausting to uplifting and everything in between. I stared into those baby blues and remembered who I was, acknowledged who I am and identified what I want to become.

I never kept track of time, as I was taught but surely I was there much longer than five minutes. Soon I was able to recognize myself again. Before I even noticed that the staring competition had ended, I was talking right aloud. My profound thoughts evolved into several mini conversations. I was laughing, cracking jokes, even flirting with that girl in the glass.

There she is! That's who I was looking for! That girl is me. That girl is alive and vibrant. She is spirited and animated. That girl sure smiles a lot. Again, that girl is me.

It didn't even come down to Perry himself. There was no question that I was doomed to be forever drawn to him but in the end it was the furthest thing from his fault. What mattered most is the way I reacted to being near him again and I didn't care for feeling the way I inevitably did in his presence.

There is no quick, perfect fix in the land of preservation but I still don't see the problem in trying to shake off the derogatory traits we pick up and shield the desirable qualities we hold. That's me in the mirror and that's you framing a picture. That's her putting a seatbelt on her child and that's them putting MSG in our food. That's how preservatives help guard what matters most. Does anybody else have a taste for crab rangoon?

KEEPING THE FAITH

Having faith is when you commit to a belief without any evidence. It's no easy task. It's being sure of things hoped for without proof or promise.

I struggled for many years with my faith in God, but that's a different story altogether. I'm happy to say, however, that in the past few years He and I have become quite close. But I digress.

Many people struggle with the concept of faith itself. Whether it's for religious reasons, maintaining faith in a relationship or even having faith that guy in the office will pay you back that five bucks he owes you.

One thing I have never battled with is the faith I have in myself. I suppose that sounds narcissistic but I think it makes me one of the lucky ones. I have absolutely nothing concrete to base on my belief that everything is going to work out for me. I haven't an ounce of proof to back this belief, but I have a ton of faith; a strong allegiance to myself.

I have no idea if I will meet the man of my dreams and fall in love all over again, but I know in the end, that everything will be just fine. I don't know if I'll end up having to adopt so many kids that we should live in a shoe, but I believe that it will all work out. I can't prove that I'll be successful in my career forever, but I have faith that it will all turn out alright. I know, I really do, that everything will eventually fall into place.

That's faith. It's pretty powerful stuff, huh? Submitting to faith of any kind doesn't always come easy but brings a sense of peace unlike anything else. In faith, there is no room for questions or doubt. It lies in the certainly of believing in something there is no absolute proof of.

I remember the times Perry asked me to have faith. It finally dawned on me that perhaps he didn't mean to have faith in him, per say, but just faith in general. Maybe that was his way of saying no matter what happens between us, we're going to find what we're looking for.

That's not to say that my faith lies in the hope of a romantic love whatsoever and certainly has nothing to do with a tall supply of male attention. Honestly, between my father, my three brothers and the Man upstairs, there will never be a shortage of men in my life. I worry not about it at all. I have faith that everything is going to be alright in the end. Getting there, to my final destination, whatever it may be, is the real adventure.

Faith provides paths for us to choose without evidence that we will find that we are looking for. But that's the beauty of it. Who needs proof when you have faith?

There are plenty of times when I'm unsure of the path I have picked, not to mention my means of getting to where I'm going. But when I find myself at a crossroads, logic will usually guide the way and the power of my conviction will keep me on track.

Do you envision your outcome? Can you play it out in your mind? What will become of you and how things will turn out? There are plenty of happy endings to be had, am I right? And don't forget about the alternative endings that may be and how you can be assured of the happiness that goes along with them.

When will we arrive at our destination? Who's to say? Keep your faith alive and you might just be there before you know it. Or just keep in mind that with a strong sense of faith, you will reach your target at some point. Life is a journey of betterment, a voyage of advancement. Mine has been an astonishing work in progress. How's yours going so far?

Acknowledgements

Mom, for believing the best of me has yet to come.

Dad, for my backbone; I've needed it.

Limon III, for showing me the meaning of drive and motivation.

MatchuD2, for teaching me the value of a reputation.

King Creole, for always pointing me in the right direction.

Gage, for believing that I've always got something up my sleeve.

E. Aloni, for your guidance.

Lee, for taking me under your wing.

Maddy, Lily & La for always having my back.

Triangle, for your support.

Perry, for loving me, once upon a time.

And for anyone who has ever stopped me in the middle of a story and told me that I should really write a book.

Thank You

CPSIA information can be obtained
at www.ICGtesting.com
Printed in the USA
LVHW090336290920
667361LV00001B/99